MW01292186

Setting changes are listed before each chapter for those who are stream-of-consciousness technique disadvantaged.

CHAPTER 1

After a phone call to main character Jock Moses tells him his best friend's father has died, he recalls when he took a trip to a Georgia hospital from his home in Minnesota

He was my father.

That was a statement both Aaron and I could make now.

Dolly had called from Atlanta to tell me her Dad had died. Dolly was Mackenzie Aaron Jr.s sister. Aaron had four brothers but only one sister.

She had brought their father to Atlanta so that he could receive special care for the brain injury he had incurred. The Aaron family had lived in Augusta for more than 40 years.

I was surprised when she called, though.

"Jock?" she inquired.

"Yes?" I wondered back.

"This is Dorothy. I brought my Dad to Atlanta because he needed the best care."

We always called Dorothy "Dolly." Funny, though, she never called herself that. After the five boys came this little doll Dorothy. She was a doll. Her soft, soothing voice, which she snared from her father, poured over you like honey on a biscuit.

"I don't know what happened. He passed away today."

The voice. So relaxed. Always.

Nothing ever rattled Dolly. Not even the death of her father.

"This can't be," I thought. I remembered back to four months earlier when Dolly told me that Mackenzie Aaron Sr. had gone shopping for his wife Alabama. She had wanted a new dress for Thanksgiving. And the elder Aaron went to find one. Alabama was nearly blind because the diabetes she had was slowly robbing her of her sight.

On the way home, just two blocks from home on the north side of Augusta, a drunk driver ran a red light.

His vehicle slammed into Mr. Aaron's station wagon which spun around before hitting the wall of a liquor store. Thinking about the moment, I could hear the glass being smashed and Mr. Aaron's body tossed around the big wagon.

The elder Aaron was a big, big man. I thought about the Tennessee Ernie Ford song, "Big John," about a huge man

HITTING THE
WALL

JOHN V. NELSON

Hitting the Wall
Copyright © John V. Nelson

INTRODUCTION

This novel is based on the real life of the author and is written for Vietnam vets in hopes that when all the sons of Vietnam War end up hitting the wall of pain in their lives they will remember to NEVER GIVE UP because there is One who will never give up on them. Who is He? Maybe you'll find the answer in this book that is meant to be an inspiration to you. For the rest who read this, believe that you can walk away from your war and then run with confidence into the future.

This story is about a man called Moses, who like his namesake- the Biblical character named Moses -spent about 40 years wandering in the wilderness. It is also about his best friend Aaron, who was like a brother to him. Did they reach the Promised Land? Wanna know what happened next? Turn the page to find out.

who saved his fellow miners from a cave in. That was a man who always thought of others.

This 6-foot-6 man was possessed of such bigness.

But now he lay in total silence.

Four months ago when I first went to visit him in intensive care in the Augusta hospital, I was first devastated and then hopeful. I remembered the week of Thanksgiving like it was yesterday, but today was March 21,1990. Earlier in the day the sun had glittered on the icicles that hung from the roof outside the master bedroom window. But now, a storm brewed outside as snow cascaded down covering the Norway pines that lined our property. Inside, a blizzard raged. As the snow fell my thoughts fell back to my final Thanksgiving with Mr. Aaron.

He had laid in silence then, too.

After convincing the nurse that I was like a son to Mr. Aaron, telling her that I had been in Vietnam with his son, I was allowed to see him.

Tubes, which seemed more like snakes taking this man's life away, carried nutrition to Mr. Aaron's now seemingly shrunken form. He didn't look like a giant in that ghost-like hospital bed.

"I really don't know anything," said the intensive care nurse. "I just came on shift and there isn't much on the chart."

I looked on the chart, filled with chicken scratching. I wondered if she was telling the truth because there seemed to be plenty of information on this 8 1/2 X 11 inch pad. But then I couldn't read this doctor's writing.

I guess I just had to trust the nurse that the hieroglyphics were nothing more than preliminary probings. Trust was not something I was good at since guarding every step as if it might be my last while I was in Vietnam.

Ever think about why doctors write poorly? My best friend Jim Behnke from high school not only had a doctor's great bedside manner but the bad penmanship to match. I always thought he should have been a doctor. Instead, he spent time researching how to make pizza more nutritious for Pillsbury in Minneapolis.

Maybe doctors scribbled in secret code so only hospital personnel would know what's going on.

I stood next to Mr. Aaron's bed.

He had suffered a head injury. I found that out. He was in a coma. That too I had garnered from the nurse. College training as a reporter had worked.

I wanted to know more. Maybe I even thought if I knew more I could make a suggestion to make him better. Or I could tell my wife Alexandra. She had worked in intensive care units in North Chicago where patients with head injuries were treated like a precious band of pearls.

As I first looked at big Mackenzie Aaron I saw a lifeless form, but I rapidly went up past the cotton sheets to his arms, which lay like pillars in white sand. Then I reached my destination.

His face.

It was his face that knocked me over like a strong March wind.

It wasn't a face of force that wanted to dominate you. Yet it did. Fathers' faces do that. It was a wise face. It was a peaceful face.

This mountain of dust which had been formed into a man 72 years before, not only filled the seven-foot bed that had to be specially brought in for Mackenzie Aaron Sr., but his presence cascaded around me also. This tower of strength enveloped me.

My friend Aaron.

Yes. I could say that about big Mac and little Mac as they were once called when Junior was a little boy. I had not known him then. Now little Mac was as much a giant as his father.

I laughed among the tears that came to my eyes as I looked at big Mac. My friend Aaron, one...no, two struggling for life at this very moment.

CHAPTER 2

A trip back in time to Vietnam where Moses and Aaron
became friends in 1967

I laughed not only because I needed to, but also because
people always laughed at Aaron Jr. and I. When you're 5-
foot-6 and pal around with someone a foot taller, people
love to rib you.

Since Vietnam both Aaron and Moses had wandered in
the wilderness for as long as the 40 years the Israelites had
about 4,000 years ago.

"Forty years?" I asked out loud. We had been friends
for a long, long time, but our paths had struggled down a
tough mountain trail, much like the ones in Nam.

Even in those times, despite the presence of death, we
laughed. The tower Aaron and the compact Moses.

Our jobs in Nam were like our personalities. Aaron was a communications specialist, sending messages through the purple majestic mountains and the green verdant valleys. He transcended power. At least his coded messages did. Since I edited not only the stories of love and anger from my correspondents for the Marine publication Sea Tiger, but also the messages from Aaron when I went on patrol with the infantry (or grunts as they were called), I was a vital link between Aaron and the men.

I was a combat reporter or communication specialist, too. Or supposed to be.

Late in our tour I was out on patrol when Aaron sent me an urgent message.

"You are in grid 0214500, Moses," he rattled over the airways into the hand-held black receiver that I had pulled out of the dusty, oil-stained green pouch that the radioman carried.

"Or at least that's where you're supposed to be," he chided.

"But do not go any farther west," he continued. "There is thick jungle and we have received information (always wondered if that information came from US or THEM) that there are heavy concentrations of Viet Cong in that area."

"So, we believe..."he started again.

"Yea, I know, Aaron," I said with a sarcastic tone. "Go east another 500 yards to grid something or other and wait for more instructions on Charlie."(Nickname for Viet Cong was Victor Charlie or simply Charlie.)

"I guess I don't need to talk to you over the phone," he chuckled. "I'll just send out messages by osmosis."

It was true about us. We, Aaron and Moses, coming from different parts of the U.S., one black and one white guy, and a foot in height apart, could communicate in a visionary way. Yes, we were separated by several miles from the compound where Aaron whistled his messages from a safe (?) bunker to where I was located along a river much smaller than the Mississippi I had grown up on, but he mixed with me like a deerskin glove fits on your hand.

We were brothers, not blood brothers, but we helped each other like brothers should.

But, we also fought like brothers. And we liked to pull jokes on each other. We had this game where we could try to fool each other through our words. Could we decode the truth?

Were we really The Osmosis Bros, Inc.? On this steamy day in February, when the water in the rice paddies we waded through felt it was going to boil not only the green rice shoots standing tall but also our feet, which were being baked in our rice paddy stomping boots.

"It is not grid something or other I want you to go to," said Aaron.

I laughed at Aaron. No, at his tone of voice.

He came from a fine family and...well...I almost thought of him as British royalty sometimes.

You know the type that always had to be prim and proper. Manners and all that. Never use the word "bloody" except in stressful situations.

"O.K. Mr. High and Mighty," I teased him.

Aaron quieted down, ignoring the reference to "high and mighty." Odd, I thought.

After a gush of wind from the receiver came through like the sigh of a Sergeant for one of his men, Sgt. Aaron moaned. I knew he was thinking this dolt finally realized you have to be specific about grids.

"Moses, you go directly 500 yards east, then head north into the LZ (Landing Zone where choppers throw you into the unknown jungle) 1,000 meters, I mean yards."

I laughed again. Meters instead of yards? Maybe Aaron did have some British blood in him.

"O.K. ol' buddy." I cracked back at him. "Then what?"

"Listen carefully, Moses," he rattled on. "Go 500 yards west and then 1,000 meters, I mean yards, south and wait for instructions; no, you better tell me what you see."

"I'm on my way, Aaron." I was thinking he made the mistakes "meters" twice. Sometimes he had the habit of making mistakes when his computer mind was on something else. It was then his concentration wavered. But I did not think any more about his error-but I should have.

The patrol moved out not knowing each step or the directions we were taking, principally because I forgot to tell anyone else. After all, I was not an experienced soldier. I was a writer, wasn't I?

After we stopped at each point, first east, then north, then west, we started south.

One of the guys in the platoon, his name was Ford, who was a very practical, but prophetic man out of Michigan (Where else would a guy with a name like Ford be from?) astutely realized what was happening.

"Man, Moses. You definitely did not lead us to The Promised Land this time. We are going in a circle, or a rectangle to be more precise."

I groaned with the inner pain of a woman in labor. Although obviously I had never been through that, I had once watched Farmer Black Colby's wife give birth to a baby when I was about 12 years old back in Minnesota, but that's another story.

I had been bamboozled by Aaron.

I had been had.

He got me.

In a flash I had been upset at Aaron, but just as quickly my temper subsided. I smiled and laughed softly.

CHAPTER 3

Back to a Georgia hospital to see my best friend's father

As I drifted back to the hospital room where Aaron's father's frame laid as still as a warm summer Georgia morning, I tried to find out for myself what condition this mountain of a man was in.

"Mr. Aaron. It's Jock Moses."

He didn't move.

"Mr. Aaron," I said louder. "It's Moses."

I would have screamed but with other patients there, and, well, it was a hospital and you are supposed to keep quiet. The word "quiet" never had been used to describe me by my teachers in school or my friends through the years. Sometimes my mouth got me in big trouble.

Always thought it was a little weird to be silent in a hospital where friends and relatives die. No, I didn't want to think that. I was going to help him get better. He wasn't going to die. It seemed funny to not scream out with the emotions welling up inside me like a car radiator about to blow.

"Don't die, Mr. Aaron."

That had been our cry in Nam. We always said there was one rule in war and that was, "Don't die."

"How are you doing?"

A perfunctory inquiry.

"C'mon, Moses, break the padlock on your feelings. You've never had problems sharing them before," I reminded myself.

"Mr. Aaron. You know you can make it."

I had ripped right to the point- fight back.

If there was a theme I kept sinking into other's minds, it was the one my own pop had given me on a baseball field long ago.

Maybe that's why I had always felt close to Aaron and his father. While his father had always risen above all hurdles, my friend Aaron had stumbled. Badly.

A funny feeling came over me. Despite the fact that Mackenzie Aaron Sr. had five sons and one daughter, none of them were there in the neurological intensive care ward.

Where were they? I thought maybe at home. After all it had been nearly three days since the accident. I guess

16

everyone needed a break from the hospital white blindness that carried one off on a magic blanket of sorrow.

Still, I knew I would have had a tough time staying away from my father's bedside during visiting hours.

But I dismissed the negative thoughts and turned back to the man who had been a tower of strength for me, but now I saw this tower crumbling brick by brick.

Tubes seemed to fly from his mouth like the tentacles of an octopus about to squeeze its victim deep under the sea.

CHAPTER 4

A trip even farther back to a baseball field when Jock was
10 and learned to never give up from his father

The sea; now that was a place I knew well. And didn't like. My father, Zebedee Moses, was a man of distinction. But he did not have the aristocratic, powerful, political nature of Mr. Aaron. What my father had was a soft, almost sweet presence which surrounded you like a net.

My father was good with a net. He could fish, from one-pound bull heads in the northern parts of Minnesota where he had lived since he came to the U.S. to the 100-pound tuna off the coasts of England and Ireland around a small section of land called the Isle of Man. But my father could also snare you with his words. Maybe that's why I always signed my name jock "z" moses.

My middle name was his. I wanted to remember his words. That's why I put my father's name in quotes so I could recall his quotes.

One of my father's favorite sayings was "Keep smilin'."

When I was about 10 years old, I had joined the Cub Scouts in Sibley, Minnesota, where I had grown up. My father and mother, Ula, who was the kindest person you could ever meet, had decided in 1940 to move the family from the British Isles to the "Land of Opportunity" as Pop called the United States of America. Even though he never struck it rich as some would look at his "catch," he did find treasure for his family.

And that was probably what he was looking for anyway- he was a pirate searching for gold doubloons for his wife and three children.

One day while we were playing baseball, which was not only the national pastime but mine too when I was young, I had that saying of "Keep smilin'" of Pop poured over my head.

That saying took on physical qualities. It soaked me like an 80-pound tuna, which I probably was that day.

In fact, the lesson I learned that day let down a curtain to this one act play and I was dubbed with a nickname.

The hard part to this lesson was that it came on my birthday, my 10th birthday. Sure you wanted everything to go smoothly on your birthday. Insanely, you wanted everything to be P-E-R-F-E-C-T.

I would even try to be perfect on that one day. Years later I could laugh because I knew I would never make it. Yet one day I think I reached 4 p.m. before I had a bad thought about my older brother whose job it was to feed our dog, Suki, and my job to clean up after our cocker spaniel, who resembled a black bear cub because his hair wasn't cut very often. Oh, well, when I tried to be perfect it was a real drag. But when you're 10 you think you gotta be.

That is where my Pop came in.

Our Cub Scout pack had progressed the last couple years. We had moved up the ladder from the initial stage of scouting, the Tiger Cub, to Bobcat to Wolf and now to Bear. We could see the finish line of Weebelo I and II ahead. We probably thought we were hardened Cub Scouts, undaunted by whatever nature threw at us. It wasn't nature that tossed me a curve that day.

His name was Custer.

In this case, unlike the historical figure, it was not his last stand.

It was mine.

Our Cub Scout Pack No. 721 was always second best to Pack 722. Funny how their number was one better than ours because that was usually how the score came out-they would knock us off by one.

Earlier in the year they had done just that with Custer not only holding us to one run, but he also hit a two-run homer which glanced off my glove in center field in the final frame to win the game.

This time, this partly cloudy day, the sun was not shining at all for our Pack 721 and was becoming darker by the inning. We had given them one run in the first inning when our tall and gangly shortstop Tom Lee, who had only one good eye, bobbled a grounder, which allowed Pack 722 to take the one-run lead.

Inning by inning went by. No one scored. We had one final chance in the bottom of the last inning. We knew we were down to our last opportunity to beat the team we had always wanted to knock on their cans.

After two strikeouts we loaded the bases with three walks as Custer developed a wild streak which 10-year-olds often have. Custer was about a year older than most of us- and much bigger. Custer had struck me out the first time up. The second time I had coaxed a walk from him.

Now.

The final time. Maybe it wouldn't be the final time we ever faced each other, but when you're in a clutch situation where all your teammates are depending on you, you have the weight of the world on your shoulders.

It's all up to you.

Do or die.

Custer's big right arm flashed up into the sky and let loose with one of his lightning bolts.

"Strike," the umpire bellowed.

Custer rocked and fired another rocket. This one sailed high. I had an advantage. I was the smallest kid on the team. I lowered myself into a crouch so there wasn't much of a strike zone between my shoulders and knees. Custer had found the space once, but missed the second time.

I looked at my adversary. It looked like he was King Custer. We used to play a game where you were king of the mountain (usually a snowdrift in the winter) where the biggest and strongest usually prevailed.

That's the way Custer looked that day.

The boy-man on the pitching mountain was not the only menacing threat that day. From the west an ominous cloud, which had so many appendages it looked like two scorpions, each with six arms and legs, was headed our way.

When Custer wound up and fired the next fast ball, that was all about I saw-arms and legs coming at me.

Zip.

Strike two.

As the storm cloud advanced over our field so did the end of the game appear to be advancing to its conclusion.

Custer reared like a wild stallion ready to attack and fired again.

Ball two.

Again he came.

Ball three.

I stepped out of the batter's box to collect myself. I remembered what my fourth-grade teacher Mr. Nelson had told me in class earlier in the year. Everything had slowed down to a crawl. This was one of those moments you never forget. Mr. Nelson watched me write a story in class. I'd start, stop, start, stop again. Cross out what I had. Start again.

This eagle-eyed teacher came over to my desk.

"Trust yourself," he said quietly. "Be confident."

So I did that day. I wrote the story with confidence trusting my own creative abilities, spilling out the details of a great football game between the University of Minnesota and Nebraska where Paul Giel, the Golden Gophers' All-American football player, scored the tying touchdown and Gino Cappelletti kicked the winning point.

That confidence was what I needed right at the moment. Consistently Custer had thrown fastball after fastball to me all day. But then this giant out on the mound did something I did not expect. He shook off the catcher's signal for this 3-2 pitch. That surprised even the catcher. He went out to talk with Custer as the rain cloud started its work, dripping larger and larger drops on all of us.

I could see Custer smile and the catcher nodded his head as the pitcher explained what he wanted to do. Two outs. Bases loaded. 3-2 count. Down 1-0. A hit would win the game and I would be a hero. A strike out would be a defeat that I didn't think I could ever recover from. Wondering what Custer was going to throw-fastball or the curve he might have-I faced the enemy.

It was that element of doubt that cost me my confidence-that trust in myself my teacher had talked about. Even though the fastball was like a clear white rocket out of one of Flash Gordon's Saturday morning serials I watched on our new black-and-white television I can still see the ball in slow motion.

Before I could even move the Jackie Robinson bottle bat, the horsehide had cracked into the catcher's mitt.

Strike three.

The rains came.

I sat down next to home plate. I had failed. I was frozen in time. I didn't think I could ever get up. The players huddled under a tree as the avalanche of water hit the field. Like 10-year-olds will do, they laughed at me.

"Look at Moses out in the water. He looks like a tuna. Maybe he needs his daddy to come and catch him."

The kids knew my pop had been a tuna fisherman in the old country.

"Yea, he looks like a tuna all right. Where's your old man?"

No one knew that my father had come to the game. He probably wanted to remain invisible so I wouldn't feel pressured if I saw him.

Although he had grown up in an area where baseball was never mentioned, he had taken to baseball rather quickly. He was older than the fathers of my friends. Their father's moustaches were black. My pop's was white. He and my mother had seen me come into their lives as a late surprise after almost raising two other kids. I was the third and the runt of the Moses family.

The smallest of a tuna fisherman.

I really looked like a tuna sitting in the puddle that used to be a batter's box but was becoming more like a roaring ocean that beat against the rocks off the coast of the Isle of Man. Even though I had never been there my father's stories about the old country fascinated me.

What fascinated me at that moment, though, was like a soft, gentle breeze on a summer's day when things were unbearably sizzling; my father breezed into the situation and drew me out of the sizzling, embarrassing water.

"You strike out?"

Then he answered my thoughts about that question which just didn't sink in that day, but I have carried with me every day of my life since.

"C'mon, Jock," said Pop, "you come out of the water."

He laughed that confident laugh of his as he drew me out of the water. Whenever my father laughed he put his whole self into the action. Just like me he was built small, but stocky. Whenever he laughed, I would have to join in.

"Those boys. They laugh at you," he said in his best accent of mixed Irish, Welsh, Scottish, Norwegian and Swedish. At one time or another the Isle of Man had been ruled by the Irish, the Scots, the Vikings plus Wales and England. The Swedish accent part came from a close friend, Vernon Oliver, who led the world in the consumption of Swedish meatballs according to my mother, who had to prepare that every time he visited us, which always seemed to be at meal time.

"You do look funny, Jock. Yes, like a tuna. But you are my prize catch."

I never loved my pop more than at that moment.

Pop was not a big man. He was five-foot-seven. I knew that I would probably be like him in stature. His scarred round face was almost as perfect as a baseball. Despite the stitches from the scrapes he had been in as a boy, when you touched his face it was as smooth as the cowhide cover of a baseball. If you would hold a Major league baseball with the "Rawlings" looking at you, you could imagine how big of a smile my father had stitched on his face. So, while he had learned to defend himself on a distant island as a youngster, he had learned a more important lesson-one that he was about to pass on to me.

"Remember, Jock..."

He poked at his eyebrows as he groped for the right words. Those wild, snowy eyebrows, that stood out like porcupine quills, ran over the deeply-lined furrows coming from his eyes that always seemed to be smiling.

He had always told me when I went to school, "Keep smilin' Jock. When something bad happens, things have a way of turning around." Now he reiterated the same stuff. Through the downpour he continued the lesson. "Remember...to keep smilin.' When you strike out it's like when you slip on the wet pavement and end up hitting the wall back at the restaurant and fall flat on your face. But you pull yourself up and go on to your next battle station? What did my father mean battle station? Later I would learn battles happened not just in war time. But that's another story.

We walked from the field to our white stucco two-story home in the small town of Sibley, Minnesota.

This town where slightly more than 1,000 residents worked and played hard. It was a short walk because we only lived a block from the ballpark.

While it didn't take long, that short walk with my father was to serve me for a long time.

The end of the lesson was about to sink into my skull just like the heavy rain that had not let up. I nearly blocked out the waterfall off the tip of my maroon and gold baseball cap. My father had given me a University of Minnesota Golden Gopher cap for my third birthday when I had my tonsils out. The cap was way too large then, but since I had grown (Yes, I had grown even though I was the smallest in my fourth grade class and now the cap fit like I was born with it permanently attached to the top of my head.

Before we had walked in the side door and come up the three steps to the kitchen, my father astutely explained what he meant by my battle station.

"See Jock. You know how to fight with your fists. I have taught you to defend yourself, but never to start a fight.

27

"What I want you to remember after I'm dead and gone is to...

"NEVER GIVE UP."

He said the last three words with such emphasis that it seemed like they sunk right through my skin into my brain.

We stepped into the kitchen. Like always my Mom was at the white porcelain stove with her back to us, cooking up another one of her specialties. Tonight I could smell it was my favorite-hunter's pie, a casserole of meat, potatoes and carrots, topped with biscuits.

"We're home, Ula," said Pop. "I stopped to see Jock play ball after closing up the shop."

"Well, you must have closed up early," said my mother, who must have read my father's mind.

"Yes, I did, Ula. How did you know?"

My mother didn't answer because she turned around and saw me. She looked hard at the cap still dripping water all over the hardwood maple walnut floor that was always spit-shined like a Marine's boots.

"The cap, Jock."

She gave me that stern and concerned look mothers have sometimes.

"Jock, you never remember what I tell you, do you?"

I must have frowned - either that or she could read my mind. Did all women react like a reconnaissance satellite and read their mens' minds?

"I just want you to be a gentleman, Jock," she added.

"I know, Mom."

"Well, get in the bathroom and clean up before you sit down."

As I walked past her with a wounded spirit, she revived me as she always did with her daily interest. "Did you win the game, son?"

I shook my head. One thing about my mother I had always appreciated. She never chewed me out for playing baseball. She knew I loved the game. She never complained when she had to wait supper until it got dark. Sometimes she had to keep it hot, for a couple extra hours, I thought. I really never knew because she never told me. I always knew I would get a hot meal.

CHAPTER 5

Looking at the families of Aaron and Moses

Would you like a hot meal?"

"What?" I said.

It was the nurse.

"A meal. Aren't you hungry? You have been here for nine hours and visiting hours are over. There was one hot meal left over. Well, actually I ordered one for you and just warmed it up in the microwave."

This kind nurse...I looked at her nameplate-Mickey...was just like my Mom.

"You bet," I said in my favorite Minnesota phrase. Only nine hours. It seemed like years.

"The first shift nurse said you were friends with Mr. Aaron's son?"

"Yea, his son and I were best buddies in Vietnam. My father has been dead for 10 years, so I kinda adopted Mr. Aaron. He's a wise man."

Everyone always thought highly of Mr. Aaron. If you took a mind trip through Mr. Aaron you would stop to view his quietness as he listened to you, then travel into his brain where your thoughts tumbled around like bumper cars in a carnival, and finally you would come to rest as you heard the sounds of wisdom tap into your brain like a soft, summer rain.

I glanced outside the windows of the hospital in this foreign land of Georgia. That soft, summer rain dripped off the roof and the tall Georgia pines reached to drink that sustenance from above.

Whenever I thought about the Aaron family, I thought about sustenance from above. They were a family that was fueled by faith in a higher power.

Anthony was the oldest. A typical first-born leader with inestimable qualities. He wasn't as tall as his father, but when he walked in a room he had a presence that echoed power. You did not compare him with others. You compared others to him. Everyone praised him from afar for his looks.

He was born for politics from the start. Just like the Irish clan, the Kennedys, who came from a bare existence as potato farmers, so had the black Aaron family who could turn back the clock 100 years to find slaves in their roots.

Miles was the second son. A well-decorated soldier from the early days of Vietnam, he had returned to help his older brother with his political ambitions. He lived the line from Robert Frost's poem which said," and miles to go before I sleep." Miles hustled over as many miles of the red, sandy earth of Georgia telling whoever would listen about the incomparable Anthony Aaron.

My friend Aaron- the third son- was a duplicate of his father in stature as well as by name. While Mr. Aaron was a wise man, I thought Mackenzie Aaron Jr. was able to take his father's wisdom and not only apply it to his own life but to other's too. His wisdom was so smooth that in Nam his nickname was "Ponds" after the smooth skin cream.

But that had changed after coming home from Vietnam.

My friend Aaron had not jumped into the political arena to help his brothers. After Vietnam he felt he couldn't help anybody, including himself. I felt badly about that because he had been a leader in Nam. While my friend Aaron's two older brothers were ambitious, both had their feet planted on the church's way of doing things. The church they belonged to was a Baptist group that realized life was teamwork between you and the Lord. At least that is the way Mrs. Aaron put it.

"While God has the horse power," she would say, " He lets us hold the reins."

Quincy, the fourth son, did not take part in the family's activities. He had moved north to the Latin quarter in New

York City. He lived on Tad Street in New York and was teased by his two oldest brothers for being "a tad off."

The fifth son I had never met. In fact, I had no idea where he was. His name was Tavish. This mystery man was only the youngest son by a couple minutes. He was Quincy's twin. While Tavish was an unknown mystery, the once smooth "Ponds" was really a puzzle. How could a man change so much?

Being the only girl in the family, Dorothy or Dolly, and small in size, she had to fight for her place. While she may have been tiny, just a few inches over five feet, Dolly packed a wallop when it came to human relations. She took charge. It was Dolly who called to tell me her father had been in a car accident.

Like a whirling dervish, she had taken over when her father had been thrust into a coma.

Three days before I had really nothing to keep me from flying down to Georgia from my home in Bloomington, a suburb of Minneapolis, where I was teaching and coaching after several years of knocking around in the minor leagues playing baseball with the Yankees and Red Sox farm teams. Still, I was a little reluctant to go.

When I called Ade Christenson, the athletic director at Kennedy High School, who at 60 years old could whip anyone younger in badminton, he knew what I should do.

"Your best friend's father from Vietnam? Sure I know who you mean. Isn't his name Aaron? And his brother is running for mayor of Atlanta. He'll be the second black mayor if he wins, right?"

I told him that it was Aaron and yes his brother was running for mayor.

"No problem, Jock. You have no coaching duties until spring anyway. We'll cover your phy ed classes. How long will you be gone?"

"I should be back for Monday classes after Thanksgiving," I answered. That would give me a whole week.

The next day was Sunday, the day of rest.

I felt the next week would not be one of rest.

I flew to Atlanta.

I had kissed my wife Alexandra good-bye, which was always my habit before I would go on long bus rides as a baseball player in the minor leagues, and told my four children- Joy, Arnold, Amber and Bryant-I'd see them in a week. I would miss Thanksgiving with them, but they understood because Mr. Aaron had been my substitute father since Pop died nearly 10 years before.

Joy, the delight of my life, was a college senior at the University of Minnesota. She was always smiling. She had listened to her grandfather Moses.

Of course, Arnold, two years younger than Joy, could be accused of grinning all the time, too. Both must have inherited that from Pop, I thought. My son grabbed some of my genes, too, because he was on the Minnesota Golden Gophers baseball team. He had hit only .214 as a freshman, but Pop's advice to never give up was something that I had passed on to my son. Arnold had that saying emblazoned on the muscle shirt he wore most of the time. I knew his sophomore season would be better.

When you described Amber, you had to kinda shake your head. A typical 13-year-old never stops spinning around you, asking for this or that or wanting to go here or there.

But like a jewel hanging around the neck of a beautiful woman which accentuates her appearance, Amber's appearance in our lives made everyone shine a little brighter. She always found ways to sparkle. She always found ways to make you sparkle. Reminded me of my older sister Beryl, who would make me sparkle when she sent me birthday cards saying my next year would be the greatest because I was the greatest.

Most of all though Amber had the ability to see the truth. Like a diamond cutter making an incision, Amber could slice through our relationship and tell me what was right.

Once I had yelled at her for not putting away the dishes. She looked at me quizzically. "Why did you yell at me, Papa? You say when you teach the kids at school you don't yell at them unless they yell at you first."

The truth stopped me in my tracks and her honesty sent me into a tract of self-evaluation.

"Sorry, honey, I'll watch it."

The fourth character in the Moses playhouse was certainly one to watch. Strong-willed Bryant had just turned six a month ago, but was always turning something over or up or inside out.

Natural inquisitiveness? Maybe, but this kid thought all things were to take apart.

When my older brother Garner, who was a detective now, was younger, he was always dismantling clocks. Once I asked him, "Are you trying to find time?" to which he must have laughed for five minutes. Well, Bryant must have inherited some of his Uncle Garner's genes because he not only wanted to know how the numbers flipped on my bedside digital alarm clock, but he wanted to look inside, too.

"We can't take it apart," I said pleadingly.

"Why, Dad?" he asked pleadingly.

"Because..." I started and then clammed up my argument.

"Because why?" Bryant pried open the conversation again.

One thing about Bryant was that he didn't let someone older or bigger shove him aside without a good reason. He taught me to consider him important. So I told him that I was not very mechanical and if I ripped it apart I might not be able to put it back together and then the alarm would not go off in the morning and then I would be late to school.

"Oh, you can't be late for school," said this kindergartner, who obviously did not grasp the earlier explanations, but certainly knew the last rule about being on time for school.

We had found a common ground. The problem and the conversation disappeared.

As Bryant romped off to discover something new to ask questions about I realized from my talk with my six-year-old son that if you take a little time to search and explore the unknown you may not only find how things go together, but also how the human race can work together.

Bryant understood he wanted to dismantle my alarm clock, but he understood I was more important than that timepiece and he gave in, not just to someone bigger or his Dad, but to getting along with someone else.

"Excuse me, sir."

I was jolted back from my dream in family land by a young stewardess (There are no old ones, are there?) who wanted my attention.

"What did you say?"

I was hard of hearing and had worn hearing aids for two years. I had needed them years earlier-after a stint in Vietnam in 1967 where artillery rounds had blasted my sensitivity to sound-but for some reason I had never admitted this loss until we adopted a Vietnamese boy named Ben in 1975. But that's another story.

"Excuse me, sir."

She smiled.

Almost like my Pop, but she was a little prettier.

"Sure, I'll squeeze you," I kidded.

Some girls would either get mad or turn sullen if a guy said that, but this red-headed gal turned red with embarrassment.

"I didn't mean I wanted to squeeze you." I tried to regroup her feelings with that sortie.

"When I was a kid my mother would always make me give her a hug or a 'squeeze' as she called it before I left for school in the morning. But the reason I always associated 'excuse' and 'squeeze' because she would say, 'Squeeze me, Jock, but you forgot to squeeze me.'"

"Oh, I see, you must have loved your mother," this sensitive stewardess sang out in Scottish tones.

"Are you from Scotland?"

"Ah, yes, you can bet your Bonnie boots I am from there. Born and raised near St. Andrews. That's where golf got started. It's the old course which was a public course granted to the citizens of St. Andrews in..."

"1552." I finished her sentence for her.

"You must be a golfer if you know that, me lad."

"I learned to play while I was in the minors."

"The minors?"

"Yea, you know, the minors. The minor leagues. In baseball you start in the minor leagues and then dream about making it to the major leagues."

"Did you make it, your dream, I mean?"

"That's a long story. I would love a cup of Irish coffee or any kind of coffee."

"Why did you say Irish coffee? Are you Irish?"

"Nope, but my father grew up on the Isle of Man and he was a tuna fisherman and they would spend a lot of time in Ireland selling their catch."

"Didn't they ever go to the east to Scotland?"

I laughed. "I understand you wished they had gone to your home country. If my Pop had done that when he was younger he might have met your family."

She smiled at the thought of that meeting. "Woulda been fine with me."

She turned to go down the aisle. "I'll see if I can find a cup of brew."

This Bonnie lass was younger than I was, but a captivating creature. Sometimes I wondered why you met the mate you did. If my Pop had gone to Scotland and we had settled there we might have been friends with her parents. She could have been my wife.

Alexandra said that there was more than one person you could love, but there was a best one. A wise man once said, "There are many fine women in this world, but you are the best of them all." That was how I felt about Alexandra.

So, as the brew appeared in the hand of this beautiful stewardess, the fires cooled as I said, "What's your name?"

"Bonnie."

"Figures," I mumbled. I had read copiously how our names fit our personality or physical features. Bonnie meant beautiful. This Bonnie had long, curly hair, partially swept over her right shoulder, big blue eyes and a huge smile that said, "I'm happy."

"What did you say?"

"Oh, nothing."

"I thought you said 'Figures.'"

"Yea."

She tilted her head to the left like a cat sizing you up.

"What I mean...your name...Bonnie. It figures that would be your name. I have studied meanings of names and yours means 'beautiful.'"

She blushed again. "Thanks," she said.

As Bonnie swirled down the aisle again, I looked outside the aluminum and steel jet that glittered in the sunlight. It was just about sunset.

CHAPTER 6

Moses spins back to a lesson at sunset from his father

When I was 13 Pop and I had taken a long walk around Spirit Lake in Sibley at sunset. The beach was hard on the edge of the water, but as you walked into the water to go swimming it became softer. I had asked my father why that was-this contrast between hardness and softness.

"Jock, it's the flowing water where you are walking- the current inside softens your feel of the sand. Here where I am on the outer edge of the water, the water has come and gone. There's no action from the water to keep it flexible."

"The water is the difference?"

"Well, Jock," said Pop, as he stroked that scarred but happy face of his," yea, sure. It's kinda like you and me."

"What do you mean?"

"Aren't we hard on the outside sometimes? But when we look at God's creation like this maroon and gold sunset or you and me, his water of life's feelings fills us up with softness."

As I skipped and sloshed through the small waves I felt the soft sand beneath each of my ten curled toes which I inherited from my father. I had inherited several treasures from my Pop. Even the toes. I jumped up out of the water. Pop caught me up and set me down on the hard sand.

"See what I mean?"

"Yea, Pop, I do. When we get mad at ourselves and at others we're like this hard sand but if we just go a little deeper we can find the softness and forgive ourselves and others. We should realize that water that gives us the softness is always within our reach, that it is always there. It's..."

"Relentless?"

My Pop had an amazing vocabulary. He always said coming from the Isle of Man he had to speak two languages-Manx, which was his own Celtic dialect, and English. He was cracking that small dictionary he carried in his back pocket right then looking for "relentless."

"Yes, it means to never give up or maybe that God doesn't give up on us. That water will always be there for us. All we have to do is admit we're thirsty and drink from the cup of God's love so..."

I interrupted. "So we become soft inside?"

"That's right, Jock."

CHAPTER 7

Landing in Georgia and heading to see Mr. Aaron in
Augusta, Georgia with a stop with another red-head in
Harlem

$\mathbf{I}$ was thankful for the memories of a sunset with my Pop when I was 13 because I forgot about the descent of the jumbo jet as it headed for Atlanta's airport. The wheels touched down on pavement. My stomach and my fear of flying didn't totally settle down, but I wasn't preoccupied with myself. As the jet taxied toward the airport's tall, silvery buildings, my thoughts were about Mr. Aaron and family.

What had happened? How was he? Was he in a coma to stay? Dolly had told me he had been hit by a drunken driver and was in a coma. When she told the story she seemed detached, so matter-of-fact. Why didn't she have more emotion in her voice?

I knew Alabama would be with Dolly. Mr. Aaron had always taken care of his wife, but when he went on trips to Atlanta, which was 150 miles west of Augusta, Dolly would take over for her diabetic mother whose eyesight was so bad sometimes she could not recognize you.

I headed for the car rental booth. I wanted to go first class this time so I rented a Lincoln Continental. The machine was white with red interior. Funny, but that's the way I had felt sometimes in Vietnam, scared pale as if I had seen a white ghost and afraid we all would be shedding red blood.

I dismissed the Nam thoughts, put them in a neatly wrapped safety deposit box, and locked them away in my mind.

As I cruised down Interstate 20 which connected Atlanta with Augusta, I wondered who would be at the house. When I called Dolly back to tell her I was coming down to see her father I had asked her how many of her brothers would be there.

Surprisingly, she had joked with me, despite the fact her father lay in a coma.

"Well, at least one brother will be here. One blue-eyed soul brother. You are a part of the family you know. We'll have a bed for you. You can stay all week if you want."

The family.

The Aaron family had not always had the importance and the clout it had now, and that influence might increase if the oldest brother Anthony was elected mayor of Atlanta.

I wondered if the papers, TV and radio would refer to Anthony Aaron as the second black mayor of Atlanta if he won the election the following April. When does the press stop counting firsts, seconds, etc. for blacks? When would it be just Anthony Aaron, another American, instead of Afro American, running for office?

Would Aaron ever become just a man and lose the adjective "black"? How long would he have to keep hitting the wall of prejudice?

And would people of Atlanta make his color the issue?

Or, would they listen to his words? We all are not created equal. We all are created differently. We all have various, exciting abilities. Those three statements loaded the bases. Then Anthony would hit a grand slam with his targeted theme. We all fit together in Gods giant puzzle.

It was obvious that Anthony used his strong religious background which he had received from his father and mother as a vital part of the campaign.

He did not set that part of his life aside. His faith was weaved into his words.

I wheeled the white Lincoln off the interstate a few miles outside Augusta. The exit sign said, "Harlem five miles."

I thought about Harlem in New York, where white people believe blacks have living conditions at their worst.

45

It was 3 o'clock in the afternoon and the alarm clock inside my head buzzed, "It's time for ice cream."

I needed the short break because the rain had been pelting at the windshield at a steady pace ever since I left Atlanta two hours ago.

As I slid into the booth and looked around, I realized I was the only white man in Harlem's coffee shop.

The biggest smile this side of my Pop and the red-haired stewardess greeted me.

"Honey, as fast as you came in here, you acts like you starvin' to death."

This waitress standing before me was a lot like my mother. Always wanted to make sure I got enough to eat. When I went into Marine Corps boot camp I weighed 153 pounds.

After nine weeks I put on 18 pounds of muscle. Still, my mother always thought I looked skinny. At 5-6, I was compact, firmly put together. I had worked out with weights ever since I started playing ball, which must have been near birth.

My mother said my first sentence was, "Where's the ball?" Actually, pumping iron started right after high school.

Maybe I knew I needed to stay in shape because if my own mother didn't try to pump me full of hunter's pie and biscuits or plenty of mashed potatoes and gravy, there would be someone like this waitress who would be trying to pop out my stomach instead of my biceps.

Her name was Silva, which was stitched on her orange-and white dreamsicle uniform. Even though all I wanted was my intended cup of coffee and ice cream, Silva made me take the extra big piece of strawberry-rhubarb pie left in the pie tin- she figured she'd adopt me as her son for the afternoon.

She was so thoroughly southern the words slowly melted out of her mouth like the name, "Honey," which she had tagged me with when I walked through the door.

"You're not from 'round here, are you, honey?"

"Well, no..."

"Well, Georgia (pronounced Jawja when she said it) is been recuperating ever since Sherman burnt Atlanta (pronounced Etlanna) when he marched through here."

Never able to stay away from the obvious question, I asked Silva why I was the only white boy in the restaurant.

"Jevver (that's "Did you ever") hear anything so silly?" she said to the cook in the back. "Honey, segregation hasn't come to Jawja. We still the same folks we always was. I was born in the Jawja woods and I'll always be some kinda maid."

I challenged her self assessment.

"Wait a minute, Silva, you have a gift of gab."

Her eyebrows raised toward her hairline. Silva had the reddest hair I had ever seen.

"You are spectacular with people. I can tell you would do well in public relations. Or you could sell houses. You know, be a million dollar real estate entrepreneur."

I stopped in my tracks, realizing I had no right to tell her what she should be doing. Advice is O.K. if you really know the person. When I taught the kids in school, I tried to remember that I couldn't help them or advise them until I got to know them.

I didn't need to worry, though, about Silva. Her strength and outward personality had a fathomless inner side to it. She had some struggling with who she was and where she was. Her wrinkled face burst forth with:

"When I was younger some of my friends said it might be nice to be white and rich. But I thought, 'Silva, God made you what you are. Did He make a mistake? Nevva. No use crine (that's "crying") because you make the most of who you are and why you were born where you was.' I like being me. Nevva wanted to be anything but me. You know what I'm sayin'?"

"Yea, I do. Make the most of what you got, right?"

"That's right, honey. I have a lot of kids and I have tried to tell 'em all that. I remember when my son, Russell, went to Vietnam, he..."

My mind backtracked to a buddy I had in Nam named Russell. He was red headed like Silva. He was from rural Georgia. Was it the same kid?

"There was this guy in Nam who I knew whose name was Russell."

I interrupted Silva, which I had a bad habit of doing to people.

"He was from Georgia, but I don't remember which town. Wait a minute. Yes, I do.

"Aaron-that was my best friend in Nam- and I were talking all night with him once. And he said he was from Harlem. We both thought Harlem, New York, not Georgia. He was red-headed like you. We talked about prejudice everywhere. Why do people hate someone who is a different color? We were drinking Vietnamese beer-Schlitz from Milwaukee didn't arrive until later in our tour- which had a picture of a tiger on it. We called it Tiger...well, you know, it was warm.

"I remember crying, not understanding what it was like for Aaron, who was black like Russell, to take the blows of hatred. I had always been a fighter because I was always the smallest one in my class at school and other kids thought they could push me around, so I knew what it was like to have your face shoved in the dirt, but I didn't know what it was like to feel constant looks of hate.

"Man, Russell had some deep trouble in Da Nang, where we were located; well, it was a little south of there near Chu Lai. He shot a guy when he called Russell a 'nigger'.

"I was a combat reporter. But I did mostly features on what it was like to be out in the field. I didn't do many administrative or court action stuff. But I had buddies who did. After that night we talked until dawn, Russell was transferred to another unit. You never know about those transfers in the Marines. Was it due to the color of your skin or because somebody hated you or what?

"But Russell was not happy to be leaving his friends. All the court trial transcript that I borrowed from my administration buddy said was that somebody from a passing truck had called out to him and nailed Russell with 'nigger' and then Russell nailed him right between the eyes with one M-16 round."

I stopped. I held my breath because tears were streaming down Silva's angular, expressive face.

I knew.

Russell was her son. Tears welled up in my eyes too. I not only felt sorry for Russell and his mother, but also for the guy who was not educated to know that you judge people by their words and actions, not by the color of their skin. It had cost him his life.

I barely got the next words out as I choked about halfway through the question.

"What happened to Russell after...?"

Silva's emotions cascaded back to her son and then switched directions to me because she knew we now had something very important in common- a love for a son/brother in war.

"After he was arrested? He was put in a stockade for three weeks as investigators checked out witnesses' stories. Everything came out the same. Everybody said the same thing. This white boy yelled, 'Nigger.' Then Russell fired and..."

She started sobbing. I didn't know if I should hold her. This was a strong woman and she bounced back to the facts quickly. She wiped away the tears with a red washcloth she had in her hand, sat down on the bench across from me, picked up a salt and pepper shaker in each hand as if to say everyone gets shook up, but if we grab on to the people we love, white or black, we can make it through the turmoil of life.

She grabbed me then. "What's your name, boy?"

"Moses. Jock Moses."

"Well, Moses, the Lord sent you here today. I have kept those feelings inside me for too long. After a court martial Russell received a dishonorable discharge.

"He came back from Vietnam in the summer of 1967- well, I suppose you know what year- to a country who not only despised the vets who fought that war but were bound to make sure each vet would know what they believed. It was like those folks who hadn't been there thought they knew what Russell had gone through. They wanted to break him. He had already snapped. But why were those folks like that?"

"I had the same feelings shot at me when I came home.

"Don't feel like the Lone Ranger, Silva, I mean, Mrs...."

"It's Cosby, Moses. "(No, not that Cosby.)

"Well, Mrs. Cosby, I was called a lot of things when I came back right after Thanksgiving and just before

Christmas about this time 23 years ago. Seems like yesterday, maybe because it affected me so strongly, just like all vets and their families. But I was called a 'baby-killer.' The pressure we were under...well, I can see how Russell broke."

I changed the subject by fast forwarding to the present. "What's he doing now?"

I wiped the sweat rolling down my forehead and into my eyes. The weather was not hot, but my emotions were sizzling.

"He's been caddying over at the Augusta National Golf Club. When you have a dishonorable discharge, jobs are hard to come by."

"My best friend from Nam that I talked about is the guy I'm going to see in Augusta, Mrs. Cosby. His name is Mackenzie Aaron, Jr. Well, actually, I'm going to see his father. Aaron's daddy was hit by a drunk driver and he's in intensive care. I'd like to see Russell, too. He wouldn't be caddying now. What does he do in the winter?"

"Odd jobs mostly."

I licked up the last bite of rhubarb pie and ice cream, swallowed the last gulp of coffee, put a five dollar bill on the red-and-white checkered vinyl tablecloth, and rose to leave.

"Do you have his address?"

"You Nawthun boys are all alike. Of course I do. Do yawl think Suthun mothers don't know where their children are? Just hold on, Moses. I'll write it down for you."

As I headed the Lincoln out of the parking lot, my thoughts raced to the Aaron family in comparison to the Cosby family.

For the most part, the Aarons had the close-knit conglomerate of caring for each other. Although Quincy, who lived in New York City, and his twin brother, Tavish, wherever he was, had separated themselves from the clan.

I had been to Augusta before, but that was when I had been in the minor leagues and that seemed long ago.

CHAPTER 8

Going back to baseball; starting a family

I had signed with the Yankees after graduating from the University of Minnesota in 1965. It was kind of a surprise signing because the Yankees were scouting a speedy shortstop named Paul Molitor and a powerful outfielder about Aaron's size named Dave Winfield. But I had four straight hits the day the scout was there. One of them was a bunt which was an art that not many ballplayers captured as a treasured part of their arsenal. After the bunt single, I stole second, third and then home with my patented pop-up slide to the front corner of the plate. That speed and daring grabbed the scout's attention. After the game the scout said he'd make an offer in a week.

I couldn't believe it. I had a couple ideas about what I wanted to do. I had become a pretty good reporter on the school's newspaper. I had thought I might try teaching and coaching but that would include returning to school for another year. I wanted a break from school at that juncture. I never imagined it would be a shot at the big leagues.

My dream had always been to be a major leaguer. Now I had the chance. I wore out a path from my folks' front door to the mail box for the next week. That game had been my last so I had told the scout to let me know at my parents' home in Sibley, about 100 miles north of the Twin Cities of Minneapolis and St. Paul, where the University was located.

When I finally found the registered letter sitting in the mail box like a glittering amber jewel, I tore it open and raced past the numbers and lawyer's jargon to where I was going to sign. It wasn't a question if. I signed it and sealed what I thought would be an exciting trip to the majors.

After signing with the Yankees, I was assigned to one of the lowest levels in baseball at that time-Class B. Today they start at Class A and move up quickly. In the late '60's and the early '70's, normally there was a slow ascent from D to C to B to A before the final two rungs of the minor league ladder at AA and AAA. I was fortunate to start at rung No. 3. Because I had played college baseball the Yankees felt I could handle a higher level than Class D, where most high school phenoms began.

I played for Greensboro in the Sally (South Atlantic) League and we had come to Augusta to play the Pirates' farm club. We were only a half game out of first place so we had everything to gain. The Pirates were in last and had settled there just like the Cosbys and the Aarons. Three years before when I had signed with the team who had won more pennants (29) than any other and more World Series (20) I knew I was with the best. That's why I had gone in the Marines.

The Green Machine was the best because my high school American Problems teacher Tom Rosandich, who had been a Marine, said so. Whatever he said I believed. This was a teacher, who if he said you'd better cut your hair by tomorrow, he meant it. Once he took a scissors to one long-haired hippie dude.

Even though I had signed with one New York team right out of college, I had wanted to emulate my favorite ballplayer, Willie Mays, who once starred for another New York team, the Giants. I patrolled center field like Mays, who I called Lord of the Flies. I made over-the-shoulder catches like the one he snared against the Cleveland Indians' Vic Wertz in the 1954 World Series. Mays not only played for the Giants, he was one. I didn't feel much like a giant and I wasn't sure what the Yankees would feel after I enlisted in the Marines after the 1965 season.

Now, three years later did the powers in New York think I was still a winner? At Minnesota there had been a tremendous baseball tradition, similar to the Yankees, under Coach Dick Seibert. He had coached the Golden Gophers to three NCAA titles in 1956, 1960 and 1964. That final championship year I had been mostly a bench warmer as a junior. As a senior, though, I received my opportunity. Our team faltered. So did I. I dropped a fly ball after hitting the wall in the first game. We lost by one run. I blamed me, but like my Pop told me, "Never give up." So, I didn't.

Maybe Coach Seibert saw I would try to run through a wall to catch a fly ball because he played me the next game.

I drove in two runs with a single to tie the game with the bases loaded. Before I stepped into the batter's box in that situation I recalled when I was 10. This time I remembered to be confident. We won and the coach told me, "You're my center fielder."

But would I be the Yankees center fielder in some town? Would it be Greensboro's North Carolina blue hills again?

It was.

When I flew out to Washington, D.C. and then Baltimore and then Raleigh, the capital of North Carolina, I almost thought I was back in the Marines.

My final few months in the service were at Camp Lejeune in North Carolina and I had travelled up to Raleigh to take in a NCAA regional basketball tourney. St. Bonaventure with burly center Bob Lanier was undefeated but the Bonnies didn't win.

Even the best stumble.

I had just read an article in the May 1968 SPORT magazine about how Willie Mays was 37 years old and coming off his worst year. Yet his team awaited more miracles.

Certainly my year in Vietnam in 1967 was my worst, but were the Yankees expecting miracles from me?

At least, my little voice inside me said, they wanted me to match the numbers I had put up three years ago. So, I was assigned to Greensboro again.

I had something new in my repertoire that summer though.

It was a sleek beautiful number. I'm not talking about a new bat I had the Louisville Slugger company manufacture. The slender, skinny legs and-all figure belonged to my new wife of a couple weeks.

Alexandra.

I had once looked up the meaning of her name.

The book with the list of names said Alexandra meant "helper of mankind."

That description was a perfect fit. She had been a nurse forever it seemed. Although she had finished nurse's training while I had been in Vietnam, her mother Rachel had once told me, "Alex wanted to be a nurse since she was three."

She had received her training in Chicago's raging riots when protestors were exploding over Vietnam and the racial problems.

Vietnam and race.

Two wounds.

One might heal.

One would never heal.

Alex had grown up in Fertile Valley, Iowa, close to the Iowa-Illinois border so she wasn't very far from home. She had three older brothers and one younger.

Her father, Alphonse Alexander (A.A. to everyone) Paxton, was a leader in the small community. His honesty was known by all who lived in the little berg of 1,034. Many feel all politicians are crooks, but folks in Fertile Valley had grown up with A.A. They knew what kind of man he was.

Alex's father had a way of looking at you. He'd rub his face with his broad, strong hands, which must have been to shake off the cobwebs of his thinking machine, and then he would ask you questions. When he asked a question he looked right at your forehead so that you almost felt uncomfortable, so that you would tell the truth.

Maybe his unspoken demand of the truth with that look was what people liked. When you think about it, telling the truth is really more comfortable in the end.

His strength was in his face. He reminded me a lot of Vince Lombardi, both in appearance and in strength of character, the former Green Bay Packer coach's favorite word.

Lombardi once said, "Character is the direct result of mental attitude. I believe that character is higher than the intellect. I believe that leadership is in sacrifice, self-denial, in humility and in the perfectly disciplined will. This is the distinction between great and little men."

At 5-8, which was the same as Lombardi's small stature, A.A. Paxton still stood tall. What else could his friends in Fertile Valley do? He wasn't a coach. So, they named him mayor.

He was always good with his hands. But then, most residents in Fertile Valley, where corn grew taller than any other place on the face of planet earth, could say they were good with their hands. This farming community needed a leader who was more than talented at tilling the dirt that was blacker and dirtier than Darth Vader from Star Wars. My father-in law, like my father, had learned a valuable lesson when he was younger. Stick up for what's right. Early in life, they used their fists. As they grew older, they learned to use their minds.

As the people of Fertile Valley watched this change in A.A. Paxton, they asked him if he would become their mayor. He wasn't sure at age 50 if that's what he wanted to do. When I told him I'd vote for him and I wasn't even in his community, he said, "Well, if a Norwegian from Minnesota thinks I should run, then I better."

Even though I had other nationalities in my blood, he always called me the pure Norwegian, thinking I was pure honest. And since honesty ranked on top of the characteristic heap, according to A.A. Paxton, he figured I was honest about my feelings and the town needed an honest man to run things. So, he said, "A-O.K." He won in a landslide, of course.

His wife Rachel came from one of the first settlers of Iowa back in the late 1700s. Her great grandfather Jeremiah Tilden had been a traveling trader, ending up near Dubuque in eastern Iowa. He came to show the Fox Indians an invention that could help them in their everyday life. It was a pencil made from the hardwood trees that lined the Mississippi River and from the lead mines which Julian Dubuque had started a few years before. Tilden wanted to share much with the Indians, to really work to communicate better with their race.

One Fox "beauty" who not only was taken by the invention but also wanted to communicate better with the white man married Jeremiah Tilden. A.A. always said he would have loved to travel like great grandfather Tilden. But now that he was mayor he thought it was time to quit talking about traveling and start doing it.

"Rachel," he said, "I can show other towns what we have to offer them and those other places can probably help us with what they've thought up to make their lives go smoother."

He was always thinking, sitting in a big brown chair like Papa Bear, trying to figure out which object could mix with another object to make things better. Once he invented a tool to sharpen emery wheels so that machinists in town could cut and polish many kinds of stone. Mr.

Paxton may not have invented the wheel, but he was sure going to try to expand the uses for the wheel.

Even though he didn't continue as an inventor, his inventive mind carried out to his kids.

Alexandra had that type of mind. Appropriately she was named after her father. My mother-in-law, who I affectionately called "the old witch," must have sensed the closeness to Alex's father the first time she laid eyes on her only daughter.

Alex could figure out a way to solve whatever problem confronted her.

Like the time at the hospital when Alex had been moved from ICU where she normally worked to the obstetrics floor because nine baby boys were born in a 24-hour period. That's enough to field an entire Chicago Cubs team.

"I welcomed the move," she told me in her long letter to me while I was stationed south of Da Nang in Chu Lai, along the China Beach in Vietnam.

"It was like going from facing death all the time to bringing life not only to all those baby boys, but also seeing the smiles of the mothers and sometimes the fathers (although often the fathers were absent without leave) who realized what they had done. A new life. Wow!

"The other day," she went on, "I almost went crazy, though. It was an emergency Caesarean section. It was a tough one, but fortunately the doctor was keeping close tabs on the baby's heartbeat which plummeted from 130, which is normal, to 40.

"The mother and father had originally decided to have the birth in a regular room without all the steel beds and white sheets. It was like a normal bedroom. But having a baby, this time, was not a normal procedure. Their physician, Dr. Flannery, quickly made his decision.

"'Set up a room on this floor. I want it spotless. We don't have time to go to the surgical floor.'"

"His words sent everyone into action. The timing was perfect. It was right at a change of shifts. So, the first shift had not left yet and the second was just coming in. Even the anesthesiologist was in the hospital. Before long the baby was crying-I think it took 30 minutes although it seemed longer- but the fuss wasn't over. The father was there. He had been waiting outside the special room that had been set up and he had come in to hold his new son.

His name was Andrew, which means strong. The terrible pressure Andrew had been in had caused a fractured skull, but as bad as that sounds, he made it. But the mother was another story. She was losing blood suddenly. No one could figure out what happened. There was no flow to the tubes carrying the blood to the mother. I looked at the father and realized he was the only new person in the room.

"What had he done?

"While everyone's eyes were on the mother, I knew I had to focus on the father. I looked down at his feet and his shoe was on a cord. The cord led to the blood supply. He had stopped the flow of life to his wife!

"'I got it!' I exclaimed. I almost laughed. I grabbed the father by the arm, pointed to his right foot and told him to move to the other side of the bassinet from where he had picked up his son. I never told him it was him who almost killed his wife. Ironically, life and death are partners sometimes. I glanced at Dr. Flannery. His face was white. He had been a doctor for 25 years and as long as I had known him I had never seen him scared. I bet you're scared at times over there, Jock, although I've never seen you scared. Well, I'll write you later- much later. Ha! Ha! You know me. Love, Alexandra."

I chuckled at that last part where she said she'd write later-much later. She wasn't a prolific writer, but when she did write, she wrote with great feeling, warmth, and emotion.

Before Alex came into the world, Rachel and A.A. had three sons Seaton, Otto and Sawyer.

The first letters of the three oldest sons spelled the Morse code for help -SOS. The trio were not only a help to each other but also to their families. Well, at least Seaton and Sawyer were. Otto was not married.

Seaton was a home developer and he had married Celia while he was in college at the University of Maine. If you were looking for a radiant hostess to greet you at a party, Celia would rank No. 1 on your list. She also made the best homemade bread on either side of the U.S.-Canada border.

They had three children, two boys and a girl. The youngest, Quinn, was a deep thinker and wise like his parents. Bart, the oldest, had a fascination for war. He was always quizzing me about my Vietnam experiences.

"Did you kill anyone? What did you do? What was it really like?"

The questions hit me like machine-gun fire, but although I answered all but that first one, I wasn't sure how they affected Bart. I didn't want him to be any more warlike. The sister in the middle of these two completely different brothers was the most beautiful girl I had ever seen-next to my wife. I would always tell Cindy she looked like her Aunt Alexandra. Like another Aunt Alexandra in To Kill A Mockingbird my wife believed family was necessary for a proper upbringing. "Pride in family" was Alex's motto. So was Cindy's. Her dream was to be an astronaut. We had a special relationship. I think she knew I didn't like war and serving your country could mean going to the moon instead of to the war.

Cindy's father, Seaton, and mother, Celia, were great thinkers. Maybe because of the huge mounds of snow that rose above the telephone wires kept them from going outside during the winter months they had time to sit and think while going to college in Maine.

Their dream was to build a place by the sea.

They had heard about Hilton Head Island, a high-top sneaker-shaped piece of land off the coast of South Carolina. The island, 12 miles long from heel to toe and five miles high from sole to top, was just the place for the Paxtons because no one else had really sunk their teeth into the gator-infested swamp land.

Seaton enlisted his brothers' help.

First, he asked Otto, who had become the richest of the brothers through dabbling in the stock market, for financial banking. Then he asked Sawyer, who was president of his own construction company, if he would be the cutter of the trees and clear the way for the resorts. Sawyer's wife, Becky, who was always figuring ways to ensnare more power and money, and used those two to gain more love and acceptance from others, cajoled Sawyer to join the project-for the wrong reasons. Becky had pushed her two children, Mogul, a powerful Olympic skier, and Cristi, who looked like she would be even better than her older brother, to the top. She would push her husband, too.

Now Seaton had two things he needed-thinking and cash. He had the hard workers in Sawyer and his men. But he probably had something he didn't want- jealousy.

The Paxtons had a fourth son.

His talents lent itself to the project, too. If Hilton Head was to become a living organism, the secret of purifying the water that seeped like ooze of the island had to be deciphered. Washington, who was about 20 years younger than Seaton, was an engineer. He had studied purifying water systems while working behind the Iron Curtain in the Ukraine, a Soviet republic. Now that the democratic processes were under way with the Berlin Wall coming down, Washington pointed his protractor west, ready to jump to a new challenge. Hilton Head Island filled the bill.

While the four boys in the Paxton family had roots in the fertile soil of Iowa, they all had different abilities. But they all held a priceless treasure they had received from their father and mother: love of family.

Love of family. I had always had the necessary ingredient to start my own loving family. I realized there were a lot of fine women in this world, but that's another story. I knew, though, Alex was the best of them all for me.

Back in 1968 Alex had to put up with a lot of junk from me. Coming back from Vietnam, I not only was not sure about life in baseball, I was not positive about life.

Being close to death so often had seared my soul and mind, although I don't believe anyone knew that Vietnam had affected me specifically. I didn't want anyone to know that I had been there. I did not come back with any of my buddies. I came back alone. That was how I felt.

Our first landlady, Mrs. "P" (for Purviance), in Greensboro did not think I was a model husband.

She was right.

Anger spilled out like muriatic acid, putting holes in whatever it touched. That year there was a barrel full of anger around. Riots were in vogue in '68. Unrest was not only in Chicago where war protestors made me feel less than human for going to Vietnam, but also the race riots raged in Watts where blacks were tired of being second-class citizens.

Above all that anger was a clear message:

Be ye kind one to another.

Man is not inherently good. Remember Cain and Abel? One of Adam and Eve's sons killed the other. Murder in the first family. From that time about 10,000 years ago down to 1968 and beyond, the murders continued, both in cutting short someone's physical life and in cutting short someone's mental properties.

We go for the jugular. Competition is bred in man where he can't stand to see anyone surpass him. I had felt that way. Once I cried when I lost five straight games of Chinese checkers to my mother when I was seven years old. What I didn't realize then was that the only person I was in competition with was Jock Moses.

How would 1968 go? Would competition be the word for me? Would Alex and I have a smooth or a stormy beginning? Would I move up in the Yankee chain? What would the effect of our families be?

CHAPTER 9

Arriving in Augusta; importance of a father in a family

I chuckled as I remembered how quickly 22 years had moved by God's drawing board. How did it get to be 1990 so quickly?

Augusta was just over the horizon. I couldn't wait to see Aaron. The son. I knew I had to go visit Mr. Aaron, but I wasn't really looking forward to seeing him. I was scared.

When I stopped at Harlem, I called the house and Stanley Aaron, a grandson, answered the phone. Anthony's oldest son had a definite Southern drawl, which his father attempted to avoid.

"They're awl at the hospital," he said.

"Which one?"

Stanley had to ask someone else because he was gone for awhile. "General," he said.

I whistled the Lincoln into the outskirts and fired the smooth running automobile, which drifted on the asphalt like it was floating on a cloud, into an Amoco gas station.

While the car was filling up, I looked at the phone book at the outside phone booth for

General Hospital. I found the address and the attendant told me how to get there.

Thirty minutes later I rolled the Lincoln into the hospital parking lot. Usually Augusta was hot. It sure had been blistering when we played Augusta in the Sally league 22 years before.

Today, though, the crisp wind of autumn was trying to head toward winter. As I stepped from the car, that blast of air almost felt like a Minnesota March wind. The only thing colder than a Minnesota March wind was one from Antarctica. The biting wind woke me up. It had not been a long trip to Atlanta but the drive to Augusta had nearly lulled me to sleep.

I pulled my overcoat collar around my neck to try to keep the warmth in the way a Penguin's father protects his newborn chick by covering the baby under his warm loose skin right above his feet.

I realized how important fathers were to sons and vice versa. Intently, I traveled the 100 feet to the glass front doors in record time.

"Thought the south was supposed to be warm," I mumbled to myself. Today was a cold day not just for the wind and temperature but also for the grave situation.

Grave? I didn't want to think that!

The corridor was quiet as I approached the admitting desk. The woman seated behind the counter was busy making out some type of report. She looked up and smiled.

I thought, "What is there to smile about? Mr. Aaron is in trouble, isn't he? Where are your tears?"

But what I said to her after her perfunctory, "Can I help you?", was, "I am Mr. Mackenzie Aaron's son, well like a son. My best friend from the Marines is his son. Can I see him?"

I saw him that day-Sunday- and the next three days, going back and forth to the Aaron home on the north side of Augusta. With it being the day before Thanksgiving I was trying to think of something to be thankful for.

In the past three days Mackenzie Aaron Jr. and I had talked a lot about relationships between fathers and sons.

"He was...is... a perfectionist," Aaron said. The change from past tense to present tense sent him reeling, hitting the wall emotionally. The tears rolled down his usually smiling face. He was a handsome man. Anthony had the movie star looks for politics but my friend Aaron had similar features. Aaron was not interested in following his brother into politics. He didn't seem interested in much of anything. He had drifted from job to job just like I had bounced from town to town in the minors. Mackenzie

Aaron, Jr. felt his importance in life was minor, unlike his brother Anthony who believed he was on earth for a purpose. Since "Ponds" was a genius at electronics he had been a TV repairman. Then he had been one-of-a-kind at another company where he ran a computerized machine no one else could handle. But he quit that job after he mastered the machine. It was odd the way he jumped jobs after being so good at them. But like me he figured something bad would happen suddenly like it always did in Nam. It was like if he knew a thief in the night was coming to kill him he would open the door to disaster rather than locking it.

"I remember one time we were painting one of the eaves on one of the properties he had," said Aaron, as he continued talking about his father who expected the best from his sons.

"I had missed painting underneath in a couple minor places, and he was just as concerned about those. 'I can understand how you missed them. You were in a hurry. But you also missed some areas on top of the roof line where the eaves receive the hottest and most wear and tear. Now, that is where you want to go the extra mile, work a little harder to make sure you put some protection on those sections. Concentrate on what counts the most. If you do that, you'll be able to do well in life with what counts most in life-people, not things. Then the parts you did too fast, the parts or things that everyone else sees, can be missed temporarily but finished later. You know I expect the best from you Junior. But especially with people.' He looked at me with those big, warm brown eyes that melted you like brown sugar on oatmeal. I've never forgotten to concentrate on people and not things because of that painting lesson. Now I wonder if he'll be able to toss me any more of his wisdom. Since we got back from Nam, I've dropped the ball when it comes to wisdom."

I swallowed hard.

Aaron and Moses. Like our biblical names we wandered through the wilderness. It wasn't 40 years yet, but I hoped we'd reach that number.

We were best friends. We loved each other. We would give up our lives for each other. How fast those years had gone. Despite the streaks of deep depression for both of us and the excursions of highly appreciated joy our concentration was on this man, Aaron's father, who was battling this blow to his brain.

The first day I had seen Mr. Aaron he had not moved at all. A tracheotomy tube was inserted into his windpipe in his neck because the hospital authorities felt his condition was serious and it might be a long time before he could breathe on his own.

But I knew Mr. Aaron. The doctors didn't.

"Mr. Aaron. It's Moses. Jock Moses."

I tried talking to him again, and again, and again. Stop and start. A lot like life. Lots of stops and starts. Mr. Aaron's life had been one of worth. Decorated in the Navy for heroism- he had never told me what for because he

73

never bragged- he had been an advocate of the little guy, which, of course, being a compact guy myself, I appreciated. On that first day there was no movement, but I told Mr. Aaron that I would be back to see him tomorrow.

I put my face right next to his red face, which clued you to his Indian heritage (Cherokee), and told him in a strong voice, "Mr. Aaron, next time I come I want you to communicate with me."

My wife Alex had told me that often people in comas can hear for days, weeks, months, even years and you don't know it. I was going on that assumption, that Mr. Aaron could hear me. But, I wanted to see a sign that he was coming back to his family, which I felt an integral part of.

The Aarons all made me feel at home. Once, Miles called me a "blue eyed soul brother," and once Dolly said, "You'll always be a part of us."

The following morning I was treated to a great breakfast of biscuits and gravy, which Mrs. Aaron tried to force down me in huge quantities.

"You're such a small boy," said Mrs. Aaron, talking to a boy of 47. Of course, mothers always think their sons are boys no matter how old they are. My mother wasn't any different.

I washed down a double portion of biscuits and gravy with a glass of Minute Maid orange juice and went to see Mr. Aaron.

While the first day it had been difficult to convince the nurses to allow me to see Mr. Aaron, the second day was a breeze. Already I was familiar, or maybe just like a spider spinning its web. You don't see such things happen, but you are aware of them later.

I hoped Mr. Aaron would be cognizant of my web-spinning, my story telling, which Mr. Aaron's second son always said I was good at. Of course, my friend Aaron would agree. When he and I were in Vietnam together, I would tell Jonathan Winters stories to my buddies to keep them awake. My favorite character voice was "Granny" Frickert which kept everyone in stitches-and awake- and alive.

For now, though, my goal was to see if I could stimulate Mr. Aaron's brain cells. Send an arrow spinning into his subconscious, hoping to hit the target and draw his brain into action. I would need to have the accuracy of Robin Hood.

"Remember, Mr. Aaron," I said, "you are the head of your household. You are needed. Your son Anthony needs your advice as he tries to become mayor of Atlanta. You have helped him get there by your words of encouragement. You used Martin Luther King Jr.'s words from his famous speech. 'I have a dream. I have a dream where my four children will be judged by the content of their character rather than by the color of their skin.' It's working with Anthony, Mr. Aaron. He believed you."

I took a deep breath and continued. I was sure Mr. Aaron would be A O.K. The sweat glistened over his forehead. His life had been blood, sweat and tears. But the extra "stuff" he put into the tree of life was bearing fruit.

But while Anthony was praised by almost everyone, he had struggled in his personal life. With the time he needed to give to his job meant precious little space for his wife and eight kids. While divorce was not in my vocabulary, it was for the wife of Anthony. A break up several years before was old news by the time he ran for mayor. The split did not harm his chances to win. Of course, my friend Aaron and I had struggled too. He helped me more than I helped him. Aaron was a leader like his daddy. After the time in the Marines, that changed.

Although Quincy chose not to live near the family-we heard he had been doing well in the music field in New York City-I kinda expected him to be at his father's bedside. He had not come yet, but I hoped he would. Quincy's twin, Tavish, was absent, too. I knew so little about him. Of course, Dolly, who did not receive much attention from her father because she was always busy preparing food or telling her older brothers what to do, didn't seem to need any guidance. At least that's what Mr. Aaron had said.

"Dolly is so independent," he had told me after I had met the family for the first time. "I never have to give her any advice. We never talk it seems. I guess she doesn't need my wisdom."

I remembered his sour face when he said that.

Yea, I thought, it was his family that spurred Mr. Aaron on. Both the Aaron and Moses families had fathers that thought of their families first.

First, the fathers supported their families. Although my pop had been a fisherman on the Isle of Man where the Vikings had once scurried around centuries before, he had to change his profession when he came to the United States.

Like MacGyver on the hit television series, my pop was a resourceful man. He used what was available. In the little town of Sibley in northern Minnesota there was a need for a bait and tackle shop for fishermen. So, he started one, using the abilities God granted him as he used to say. With that half-moon scarred smile of his, he would melt the butter on the cinnamon rolls he also sold in the morning. My mother made those, and along with the steaming coffee the Norwegians and the Swedes consumed, his bait and tackle shop was half fishing equipment and half restaurant or meeting place. The floors were slate from a Vermont quarry that he had seen when he first came to this country. He had travelled from New York through the Green Mountains. The walls were knotty pine from the trees of the White Mountains to the east across the state line from a hospitable town called Haverhill, New Hampshire. He had loved the pines. I guess that is why he ended up in northern Minnesota. Pop's Shop, which is what he called it because he liked my pet name for him, was a comfortable place.

My pop was a comfortable man, like a sofa is when you lie down to watch a baseball game between the Minnesota Twins and the Boston Red Sox from Fenway Park.

While Mr. Aaron had lived most of his married life in Augusta, Georgia, he was born and raised in Ponce de Leon, Florida.

He had met his wife, Alabama, there while they were in high school.

"I was walking down the street to school one day," said Alabama, as she joined me next to her husband's hospital bed.

"I was with my girlfriends. I looked over across the street and there were a few of the boys standing on the steps by the front door of the school. This one boy not only stood taller than all the rest, but also he was the handsomest one there.

"He looked at me as I walked past him. He nodded probably because I had not been able to take my eyes off him. I was thrilled.

"Later I asked one of the other boys who was with him, who I knew, to ask him if he would meet me for a Coca-Cola at the drug store. We have been sipping cokes ever since."

Suddenly she stopped. Her eyes, which had gradually deteriorated due to her diabetes, squinted as she tried to see her husband's formerly handsome face, now twisted by the accident.

"I don't know what I'd do without him," she said.

Mr. Aaron had always been a mountain to his wife. Not just a physical one, but an emotional one.

But, he was like that for everyone. He had wanted to be in politics when he was a younger man, but for a black man in the south in the forties, that was impossible. You were lucky to be able to vote. In 1947 when Aaron, Jr. was six months old, it was reported 13-16% of black folks were registered to vote. Still, Mr. Aaron did not battle the system outwardly, which his son Anthony could do now, but rather he quietly grabbed what rungs of the ladder he could ascend and climbed them one at a time.

My friend Aaron came in and sat down next to his mother. His usually strong face, which was nearly a duplicate of his father when he was younger (I knew that because I had seen the Aaron family album.), was contorted with grief. I saw fear in his eyes, an emotion I never saw in Vietnam.

"Scared he's going to die?"

"Yea, Moses, What would I do without him?"

The soft, blue chair creaked as my friend Aaron moved it closer to his mother. Maybe he realized the time of passing for his father was near. Why did he say what his mother said? Was it because he felt his father was not going to recover? I couldn't accept that. Aaron was a person who accepted what came his way in life. I never did. I was a fighter.

Wouldn't you think that Aaron would be the fighter and I would accept life as it strolled my way, moved in, and raced on?

I mean, Aaron was black and I was white. Don't things- in life, that is- go better for white folk? In our relationship, Aaron was the stronger one. At least in the Marines it was that way. Later in civilian life I tried to be the strong one, but he never was very good at accepting help.

But Aaron was a leader in our relationship in the Marines, whether it was on base or off base.

CHAPTER 10

Who's the leader?

The base of my thoughts left the hospital and flew back in time to an all-black bar in Jacksonville, North Carolina.

It was right after we had returned from Vietnam.

Fortunately, and unusually, we were sent to the same base in Camp Lejeune, N. C. Usually the Marines brought you home alone and sent you back the same way. Then the last few months you trained other guys to go to Vietnam.

Aaron had come home a week earlier than I had from Nam. He got married on his 30-day leave to a gal named Madeline, who became a quick favorite of mine. Maddy was from Augusta, too. She made the best breaded pork chops you ever sunk your choppers into and her Johnny cake or corn bread was heavenly. Put a little tab of butter in the middle of that Johnny cake and pour a heap of honey on that fine delicacy and the whole piece would go down smoothly like a greased sled on an icy Minnesota hill on a brisk January morning.

Back in 1968 Maddy did not specifically have high expectations for her husband. At least not that I saw. She was just happy to be married to my friend Aaron.

But that changed later. But that's another story.

At Camp Lejeune the guys who were not married lived in a barracks area while the married fellahs lived in little homes in another area. But whenever we could Sgt. Aaron and Cpl. Moses found ways to spend time off base together.

One of those times was a little scary.

At this little bar in Jacksonville, all the super splibs (leading blacks) congregated. That didn't stop me from going with Aaron. While I didn't know what it was like to be black, I did know what it was like to be the lone person of a color walking into a building.

The lone white guy.

But, like I said, that didn't bother me.

"Sure you want to stay here?" asked Aaron with those high eyebrows of his when he searched your eyes for an answer. Aaron had a way of not listening to your answers and looking into your eyes for the real feelings. He shouldn't have been in artillery.

Better he should've been a lead interrogator. No one would have escaped his gaze. He could glean the truth from you like no one else I knew. I mean, you had to tell him the truth.

"No problem," I lied.

"Yea sure," said Aaron, already seeing what I really meant.

"If you want to stay so bad, then, let's at least find some Temptations' sounds to upgrade your mood."

Aaron knew I lobbied for the Tempts' songs to be played whenever we went to a dance. "My Girl," which was the No. 1 single in 1965, was my favorite.

He knew.

"My Girl, right?" said Aaron, without waiting for an answer. This guy had recon waves like my mother. I was a little bothered he could read my mind. I mean, I wanted an edge on my best friend.

I thought, why do I feel I have to be better than my friend Aaron? We are not in competition. But I still fought to reach the top of the mountain, like when I was a kid and trying to knock Custer off the mountain of snow to be King of the Hill. "I've got sunshine on a cloudy day," came filtering through the juke box as the Temptations music settled over the room like a smoke screen.

"Thanks," I yelled across the haze-filled room, that looked more like a Vietnamese building that had been bombed by our artillery than a bar in the United States. There weren't too many places to go off base. You could check out Frankie Avalon and Annette Funicello at the latest beach party movie or you could go to the bars.

The paint was not just falling off the walls; there were no walls in places. You could imagine that 155mm artillery shell rounds had been hitting the wall with regularity. There was so little light in the place it was hard to see who was next to you. And it was still early evening outside. It's true that Marines are always the first called in to storm the beaches and make the landings. Or is it the other way around? It was also clear that some Marines liked to hit the bars early, like Aaron and Moses.

Aaron nodded his head as he started a conversation with a girl near the juke box. He was always friendly to everybody. Sometimes that got him in trouble with women, because they thought he was coming on to them. Of course, being tall, dark and handsome helped, too.

The guy next to me at the bar stared at me, then growled, "Yeah, man, shut the .... up."

"What's your problem?" I growled back. Ever since Nam I didn't take any crap from anybody. "Why did you say that?"

"You don't belong here, man."

"I get the picture, but you don't." I felt I belonged wherever and whenever I wanted to go in the USA.

"Oh, yea. I'll tell you what I do get. It's you by the throat."

He snatched at me and grabbed my white Munsingwear Grand Slam golf shirt.

I looked in his eyes. Hatred.

Not for me, though. Hate for white honky.

I watched his hand go in his right pocket.

Knife?

Gun?

"Let's go outside and settle this," he said.

Would settling be dangerous? More dangerous than Nam? The same?

Like many times before, my friend Aaron intervened to lead me down the right path. This time like always he was emphatic.

"He's not going anywhere."

From across the room he had sensed the confrontation coming, sized the situation as potentially dangerous, and moved in at the right time. It wasn't the first time he had done that. He had a way of solving problems.

"This is my friend Moses. We were across the big pond in Nam fighting for you, brother. Now leave him alone, dig?"

This dude's eyes got awfully wide. They were so wide you could have seen the Grand Canyon reflected in them-almost. Aaron was an imposing figure.

With his Afro bouncing up and down like a bobble head doll, this interloper between two friends backed away from us, not taking his eyes off Aaron.

"Sure, man, I can dig it. Whatever you say, man."

When I think about that incident now I know I was ready to go into the scrap no matter what the consequences.

Dumb? I suppose. I guess I didn't care enough about life then.

However, Aaron counted the cost-his friend- and not only knew it wasn't worth the price, but also was smart enough to figure out a clear avenue out of the mess.

Always the problem solver. That was Aaron. And Aaron had to face the everyday racial problems that mostly white America threw at him.

Some might say this Aaron was not only facing a mountain of prejudice, but also had enough guts to climb to the top of the mountain.

But like the eldest son John in James Baldwin's "Go Tell It On The Mountain," Aaron was the one chosen to follow in his father's footsteps. Aaron's father did not consciously "choose," but he did name his third son "Junior." And whether the father sensed it or not at birth, he wanted someone to carry on his first name, too. Maybe it was because he felt older; maybe he felt mortal. Mackenzie Aaron, Jr., had many of his father's characteristics.

Mr. Aaron and his third son were almost made from the same quilt.

Each of them had similar bents- both good and bad. Mr. Aaron's benevolence stretched far and wide in his community of Augusta and gradually spread to the state capital of Atlanta. He was not a rich man. No blacks growing up in the sands of Florida in the Roaring Twenties were rich. While many whites somehow survived the depression in the next decade, not many colored folks-as the blacks were called then- did.

But Mr. Aaron had survived.

Maybe that was why I was drawn to this third son in Vietnam where we first met. And that was why I chose Mr. Aaron as a substitute father when my own father died. Mr. Aaron became a postman in Augusta after serving his country in World War II. He brought his first two sons there with his wife, Alabama, who had gotten down on her hands and knees and scrubbed hospital floors when she was young to help her family make ends meet, but who had risen to walk the floors as a licensed practical nurse in a small rural hospital.

That was in Ponce de Leon, Florida, where hope always springs eternal. At least that's what she always said.

"Jock," she would say to me, "since you're almost mine anyway..." Then she'd pause and try to think of something that would stick with me forever. She knew how to reach me because I always got nailed with her thoughts. Her hammering was on target. She was like my mother. Shed tell me to be a gentleman and take my baseball cap off when I come in the house.

Then she would continue.

"...You and Junior got to be more careful. You come home through that driving rain half drunk. You were lucky that God almighty didn't strike you down with a lightning bolt."

Mrs. Aaron always put the adjective "almighty" after God and pretty soon you thought you couldn't use one word without the other. She made her point, though. When I was out partying after Vietnam, I thought I was celebrating being alive after a year in hell.

I should have realized that I could have just as easily been struck down drinking and driving as I could have been facing a walk through a mine field in the dead of night in Nam.

Did I believe that God was almighty? I heard Mrs. Aaron. But I wanted to believe it for myself. Still, I knew God had listened to my mother's pleading prayers and brought me home alive instead of in a pine box.

I had wanted to go to Nam, not to kill gooks as some of my American buddies said, but to stop the Communist insurgence, the stomping of the little guy, the skinny South Vietnamese eight-year-old girls like Nuk with a dimple in her cheek and a cigarette in her mouth, by the big red machine.

While Mrs. Aaron was more open with her advice, Mr. Aaron, a lot like my father, dealt out his suggestions like a Mississippi Riverboat gambler. He bided his time and when the time was ripe, he would deal you the right cards so you would see by your own experience what worked and what didn't.

Like the time my friend Aaron and I were painting the garage. It seemed the Aarons were always painting something. Sometimes I wondered if they weren't related to the Italian artist Michelangelo who painted the Sistine Chapel from 1508 to 1512, with titanic figures which chronicled the beginning and fall of man at Creation to the destruction of man at the Flood.

Both Mr. and Mrs. Aaron knew these stories, believed them implicitly, but more importantly incorporated them for themselves.

On one hand Mrs. Aaron warned her son, Aaron, to watch out for the golden calves in the world. On the other she told me, Moses, to watch my tongue. Unlike the reserved Biblical character Moses, I usually let my fiery temper and big mouth get me into trouble. Being 5-6 I usually was at a disadvantage with any protagonist. Ironically, my friend Aaron, who could have run off at the mouth and gotten away with it due to his 6-6 stature, was the quiet one.

Just as insightful as his wife, Mr. Aaron delivered the mail on time to the both of us. He knew the difference in the two of us. He had a way of watching you first. Then he'd join in, showing you the best way to do something, then stepping away after he made sure you had viewed the correct method. So, anyway the garage's windows needed to be painted. We started sanding off the old, which was all right to begin with, but when we started to paint the trim, Mr. Aaron stepped over to an adjacent window.

Both his sons-I always included me as one of his sons since the twins Quincy and Tavish were not around-stopped. Here came the lesson.

We knew.

Calmly he took the roll of masking tape from his back pocket on his coverall jeans that he felt most comfortable in and applied the tape to the inside corners of the four panes that made up each window. Then he took a brush and dipped the brush slowly into the paint and painstakingly stroked the white paint on the trim.

Calmly, slowly, painstakingly. Words that described Mr. Aaron as he painted a garage window and also depicted a way of life-something the younger Aaron and Moses had not discovered yet.

The elder Aaron knew that.

But I think he also believed that someday we would remember. This man, who was the son of a preacher man, believed we would take heed to the right way, the right path the Lord intended for us.

He would wait patiently for that time. Both Aaron and Moses-who were brothers in the Bible- knew in their heads about God in the Old Testament scriptures. But accepting what He planned for them was not easy. My friend Aaron and I were not any different. We didn't have the same mother, but like Aaron and Moses in the Bible who had depended on each other through 10 plagues in Egypt we also depended on each other like brothers. Like them, we depended on each other for our lives.

My friend Aaron and I had wandered through the desert for nearly 40 years since Vietnam and had searched for answers from that time, never seeming to find them, wondering about not only what happened in that Asian country but also back in the world of door knobs and flushing toilets-in the United States where he and I were tossed out like yesterday's garbage.

CHAPTER 11

Mr. Aaron lifts his arm to give Jock hope

That day, though, the day before Thanksgiving, we realized that we might be facing the death of Mr. Aaron. We felt like garbage. I was a fighter, all right, but I knew I couldn't face this foe -death- alone.

I threw out the garbage that floated in my mind and I came back to reality. Yes, it was the day before Thanksgiving. I needed to find some reason to be thankful. Being in the hospital didn't seem to be the right place to be thankful. I mean, usually people die there, don't they?

I tried to dismiss those negative thoughts. I had four kids born in a hospital, so there was life there, too.

"Mr. Aaron, I got to go now. I'm sure there are big preparations for tomorrow. We'll be praying for you to get better. Squeeze my finger if you can hear me, Mr. Aaron."

The second day I had asked him to do that and I thought he had responded. But I wasn't sure. Maybe it was all in my dreams.

Today he definitely squeezed my finger. My heart soared.

Life.

Something to be thankful for.

I would tell the whole family. "I'll be back tomorrow after we gobble up all the turkey."

Then as I went out the door, I looked back at this neatly kept room with doctor's notes scribbled on charts, with venetian blinds keeping out some of the light that seemed to want to reach in and lift Mr. Aaron's spirits.

The message I received at that point had nothing to do with the nurses and doctors or with the light that seeped in to lift anyone's spirits.

The message I received seemed to come straight from heaven itself.

Mr. Aaron raised his right arm, the non-paralyzed side but up to now immovable except for one finger. Mr. Aaron raised his right arm as high as it would go and he waved good-bye.

Tears welled up in my eyes.

Yes, I screamed inside; he's going to be all right, I thought.

He wasn't talking verbally, but that one movement was the most powerful communication I ever received from him.

The will to live. But I knew God would decide if he lived.

I must have flown down the steps -I didn't like elevators- because I nearly knocked over a little old lady at the bottom of the four flights of stairs I raced down.

She was just opening the door on the first floor. I skidded to a stop but I bumped the heavy yellow-painted door slightly and her hat was sent spinning to the floor. It was a soft brown velour hat with "Birdie" written in script across the front. My attention to detail was amazing sometimes. Anyway I picked up her hat and handed it to her.

"Sorry, ma'am. I was in a hurry to tell someone the good news about my best friend's father."

"That's O.K. sonny. I'm happy for you."

I noticed that her gold-rimmed glasses didn't hide the gold flecks that sparkled in her eyes. Her face seemed to have crow's feet or smile wrinkles, as I called them, just about everywhere.

Half an hour later I parked my rental car on the street across from the Aaron home on North Fifth Street.

The homes were neatly squelched together in this neighborhood. Stucco homes like this one were similar to the one I had grown up in Minnesota. These houses were all tossed up on higher ground, though, where the lawn we

94

had was flatter than the crepe suzettes my wife made on special occasions. As I looked at the hilly landscape, I thought of the glaciers that had rolled across Minnesota and Wisconsin and how many people thought there had been millions of years of evolving to create the world.

I didn't believe that. Mrs. Aaron didn't either.

Like she always said, "We're all related back to Adam and Eve, about 10,000 years ago."

That's how she looked at all people and the Creator she believed in. We were all important or he wouldn't have created us and he could create us and the world in six days just like he said. Being a nurse it was good she had that attitude. Mrs. Aaron was not going to let racial difference cut between relationships.

"Is that you, Jock?" she asked as I walked in the front room. She was sitting in a wheel chair because she had trouble with her legs as well as her eyes. "Yes, it is, Mrs. Aaron. Something smells good already. I love your fried chicken and I know I smell some of that. What else is going on in the kitchen?"

Their house was simple- full of stuff from nearly 54 years of marriage. The house had a small front room. But the focal point was the gargantuan dining room where folks could gobble up the goodies prepared by Mrs. Aaron or Dolly or Mr. Aaron's sister Mary, who had come up from Florida to be by her brother. In the past when I heard stories of Mrs. Aaron's children for the first time, I marveled at how she could cook, eat, and tell stories at the same time. Her life revolved around a platter of chicken. That life was her husband and her kids. Now she needed help. It was sad. I guess I thought life and mothers went on forever. I snuck in the kitchen. I closed my eyes and took a minute vacation. Tomorrow I envisioned there would be bacon and sausages for breakfast. But now I could smell not only Mrs. Aaron's Georgia fried chicken-better than Kentucky Fried Chicken- but also Kentucky fried steak with four kinds of vegetables. As I walked through the doorway into the heaven city of smells I saw the corn, the beans, the carrots and my favorite-beets. There were a couple of pumpkin pies baking in the oven when I bent down to see through the steamy window in the front door of the stove.

When I was a boy, my pop would always ask my mother at the end of the meal, "What kind of pumpkin pie we have tonight, Ula?" My mother would smile and bring on whatever dessert she had prepared. Sometimes it was pie. I guess I grabbed my love of pumpkin pie from my pop.

When I entered the home, Dolly was talking to a man who I didn't know. He was dressed like the peasants dressed in the old countries of Europe 200 years ago. A tattered black hat in his hand, a wrinkled gray shirt buttoned up to his neck and an old black overcoat two sizes too big. Mr. Aaron had a fleet of cabs which he had acquired over the years to supplement the family income when he was a postman. After he retired I think he only kept those cars rolling so that these guys had jobs.

I remember when I had been struggling to find the right job. I had quit baseball in 1975 and tried my hand as a golf pro for a year, then tried sports writing for another year before heading back to school to obtain my teacher's license. After obtaining that piece of paper, I had been a substitute teacher and couldn't find a full-time job. We were so poor at that point we had to sell important items like television sets which meant we had to go next door to watch TV. My next-door neighbor, Dick Bohmer, who was a widower, kept Amber on a track from our house to his and back. He said he couldn't possibly eat up all the groceries piled up on the table. This coming from a guy who was 6-foot-4 and 250 pounds. Dick had retired from the Minneapolis police force. He was a very gentle force in our lives as Amber would bring back a sack of lasagna, taco pizza, lemonade and a bag of trail mix with nuts, raisins, dried bananas and stuff like that.

Mr. Aaron was like Mr. Bohmer. Both grew up in a big tough city. Both had big hearts.

My mind drifted back to the Aaron home. I looked at the director of the moment. Dolly had to find out what her daddy owed this man so she could pay him.

Mr. Aaron's oldest son Anthony had a big heart like his Daddy. Anthony had opened wide the door for me with the same flare and touch demonstrated by the young Spanish bull fighter in Ernest Hemingway's The Sun Also Rises.

Even though he was a black man in a white man's world, Anthony's emotions told you that he had a purity in his line. He did not react with a boisterous spirit to politics like many politicians, but rather he calmly and quietly took charge of the strength his father and mother had passed to him in a line of a people, who were black, but more importantly knew they were put on this earth for a purpose.

"C'mon in, Jock. It sure is good you're here." Sometimes people say those words and don't mean them. Anthony meant them. His eyes were full of warmth.

While Dolly busied with paying the taxi cab driver, Miles and my friend Aaron smoothed over to my side. These two were very close. Each gave their big brother his rightful place without jealousy. I didn't think Dolly did because she was always trying to take over the business of the family, but maybe she felt her older brothers were just too busy with their own lives. She did not have a family of her own. With Anthony's eight children and Miles' and Junior's two girls each, the brothers' attention could be diverted, she probably thought. But when your father hangs on to life like a mountain climber, your thoughts are all in one direction.

"What's happening with our father?" quizzed Miles. He instinctively knew that I had been at the hospital. It had been three days since I had come to Augusta and it was like the outside son telling the inside sons what was going on. But I didn't really feel like an outside son even though Mr. Aaron wasn't really my father.

I told Miles about the wave at the end of my visit with his father. "It's a beginning," said Miles, who had always been upbeat, a good soldier in Nam and after. Miles had spent some time chasing a dream as a singer. He had a captivating voice, which had mostly smooth tones like Lou Rawls. If he had been white, he would have been another Georgian's spokesman when a certain peanut farmer ran for President and made it. But Miles would have turned even Jimmy Carter down even if asked. He was a loyal family man.

CHAPTER 12

*After back from Vietnam, Moses headed from the west
coast to the east coast*

Loyal.

Funny how that word crept into my mind since Nam.
Aaron and Moses were loyal to each other, both then and
now. But not many others had been to the two of us since
coming home.

We had struggled because of the disdain we faced from
the American people who were ingrained with success and
turned aside the failures. Even taunted them. Like the time
I flew home from Nam right before Christmas 1967. We
had stopped in Okinawa and Hawaii and then finally
arrived in the U.S. at El Toro, California. I got off the
Marine transport plane and kissed the asphalt and uttered,
"Thank you, God, I'm alive." Soon after that utterance I
questioned the statement about life and death. Not just for
me, but for what others thought I had done. I grabbed a cab
at El Toro's airport to head for L.A. 40 miles away. After

arriving in the airport I realized I had left many of my photos back in a bag at El Toro. Somehow the cabby had not put that one bag of my memorabilia in his trunk. I wondered if I should go back to retrieve the memories. My thoughts at that time were clearly toward home, not backwards to the jungle. I tried to drown my sadness at the loss by guzzling as many Schlitz in a row as I could before my plane left for Minneapolis.

A man at the airport bar noticed my uniform, which blared a mournful tune like the one playing on the juke box in the corner. "Sunshine came softly through my window today. Could've tripped out easy, but I changed my ways. Superman..." Superman? Oh, no, I had not been a Superman in Vietnam. I had wanted to be. I hadn't gone there to kill gooks, but to help little girls like Nuk feel there was a chance to live without bombs reigning from heaven- or was it hell? Eight-year-old girls with dimples should have that opportunity, shouldn't they? The man next to me asked me if I was going home.

"You bet." I said that with a false, cheerful tone." Just back from Vietnam?" he asked. "Yeah, I arrived a couple hours ago." He asked me when my plane left for home.

"Still a couple hours, I think. I'm not sure," I said, funneling myself toward a drunken stupor.

"Let me see your ticket," he said.

I fumbled around and found it. He grabbed it and announced it would be a long time before I went home.

"Listen," he said, "I would like to show you how I feel about you guys. You deserve to be welcomed home in the right way." He added that he had some beer at his place. Did I want to come? I said sure. Didn't I deserve the best after going though hell in Nam?

What I didn't know at the time was that the next couple hours would turn out to be as much of a hellish memory as my previous 13 months in Nam.

He led me out to the parking garage where we climbed into a brand new Honda. Japanese, I thought. I would never buy a foreign car. I was proud to be an American and I would buy a Chevy or a Ford. My first car had been a '57 Chevy, which later became a classic. I ended up selling the car for $200 when I blew a rod right before going to Nam. I remember standing beside a huge red, white, and blue American flag which hung on the four inch circumference steel pole my pop had erected in our front yard. The photo showed Alex and I standing in front of the pole with the butterscotch and white colored Chevy in the background. I longed for home.

"Well, Marine," the guy said, trying to start a conversation, "I bet you got a lot of nookie over there, eh?"

I had spent a week in Japan on R&R (Rest and Relaxation vacation) and tried to have as good a time with as many girls as possible. I guess I thought I might never get back to Alex to marry her and did not want to leave this earth a virgin. I rationalized I might be killed after returning to the jungle.

But the jungle I faced was not just one of the physical variety but also of the mental class.

Kinda strange I thought. His conversation went to sex right off the bat. What is this guy anyway? He had hardly any hair at all. Wispy I'd call it. Big eyes that seemed to continually search for answers beyond your words. But he was looking for something else. I didn't remember the drive to a Spanish style house on the beach, which I didn't notice until the next morning. The couple hours stretched into more than I had anticipated or wanted. He got me the beer. Then he started to talk. "So, you did your good deed for your country?" I nodded my head, but I got up and headed for the door. "Listen, thanks a lot, but I wanna go home now." He grabbed me gently, sat me down on the couch and continued the conversation; this time the talk turned down an ugly alley. His talk of make love, not war continued. "What did you do over there? Probably carried a gun ready to kill innocent victims at will. I bet you have a long list of women and children you killed." I protested, which was a mistake. I should have turned in my fastest time in the 100-yard dash and gotten out of there.

"You're only guessing. You don't know what you're talking about."

Even though this was California, this house had a fire place. I walked toward the opening to try to figure out what to say next. To clear my head. I never found the opening and I didn't clear my head. I felt a sudden rush behind me. He picked up a poker and banged me over the head. Before I hit the floor and went unconscious I heard him brand me.

"Welcome home, baby killer."

In the softest voice I could imagine he blasted me with the loudest condemnation I had ever received or would ever receive. When I came to it was dark outside. The man was gone. I wondered if he had stolen anything. I looked through my billfold. Everything was in its place, including the ticket home. The final accusation before blackout haunted me, though.

Although I had fought a war against men who I didn't know, I somehow realized I was battling not only against this man but also within myself.

Was I a "baby-killer" as he suggested? Had I done the right thing to go to Vietnam? I went as a Good Samaritan, didn't I?

The booze took over at that point as the liquid drug hammered me into a semi-hallucinatory state, which sent me drifting back across the big pond as we called the Pacific Ocean to the little figures that dotted the landscape of the Oriental world in Vietnam.

Splashes of people sauntered into my foggy filmstrip as my mind rewound and paused before starting again.

The dreams.

Some were full of black horror and some were decorated with the exhilaration -at least for me - of a first white snow in Minnesota.

Black and white. The colors of Vietnam were black and white in the bad and the good and they were red and white in the blood and the flesh. We were men, young men to be exact because the average American fighting machine came in a 19-year-old package.

Although I was five years older, I was not fully mature. But, what I was forced to do was become a big brother to a lot of those "kids."

While I had grown up as the little brother and had very little experience as a leader, suddenly I was expected to be one. No one told me that I had to be one, but it was understood since I was older in years, I was smarter or more intelligent.

I think at that time the two words meant about the same. But those two words are as different as black and white.

Intelligent means you were given the brains to start with.

Smart means using what you were given.

Big difference.

Although I did know the difference in the meanings of those two words, I did not apply either word often enough.

Today the beer commercials go to big expense to tell you that drinking and driving don't mix. Intelligent, yes; smart, no. Some guys should never start, like a guy named Moses for example.

Miles and my friend Aaron still did, but I had quit nearly 20 years ago after coming home from a game drunk. I was a baseball player in the minor leagues then.

Climbing the ladder in the minors used to be as slow as molasses rolling uphill. Twenty years ago it was easy to be discouraged by your lack of movement toward the big leagues. I was no exception.

With a short stint the year before my two years in the Marines began in 1966, I had come back to the same town as before-Greensboro, N.C.- in 1968 and was not happy about that. My year showed it. After hitting .311 in 1965, my average in 1968 started on that high level but then I went into a slump the last part of the year before ending just over that magic .300 level by three points. So, in 1969 I returned for my third year in Greensboro. Fish and relatives may smell in three days but so did Greensboro. I looked to the bottle for answers.

Without a doubt I knew I could play on a higher level. I had shown that before Vietnam. But what did I do? I sulked and my batting average sank. Personally I sank, too, heading for the bars after games. My lifestyle hurt my play and then my lack of production on the diamond turned me back to my degenerating lifestyle. I was in a cycle, a tornado that had me in its grasp.

Alexandra didn't complain. She never nagged. Our first daughter, Joy, was born in 1969, so Alex buried her disappointment in me and turned her attention to a more joyful occupation-mother.

Although I loved my wife and blond-haired, chubby-cheeked little bundle of joy, I really did not show much tenderness the first couple years. I was busy trying to forge

106

out a career in the game I loved. When I think back now, I realize I loved baseball more than anything.

Crazy as it sounds I did not give my best on the field for that love. There was a simple explanation for my play. My life off the field contributed to a downward slide from 1968 to 1970.

In 1969 my play degenerated even farther than it had been the year before. My batting average dipped even lower to .294. The speed was still there, but my judgment on the bases showed the state of affairs I was in. I would always go for the extra base, daring the opposition to throw me out. There is a rule in baseball to never make the first or third out at third base. I broke that rule several times. The manager at Greensboro was different each year. The one that I had before Vietnam had moved up the ladder while I was dodging bullets for a year. Each manager saw the speed and was willing to give me a longer look because I could run like the wind.

In 1965 I had stolen 60 bases, and I was able to keep close to that figure when I returned from Nam. But with batting marks slipping my opportunities to steal dwindled. Still, I swiped 52 and 43 the first two years back.

Finally it was my refusal to listen to reason that resulted in a demotion to Fort Lauderdale for the 1970 season. Greensboro had been Class B, which was not the lowest rung on the ladder.

CHAPTER 13

At the bottom where another lesson hits home from a
father figure...and insight from a caring teammate

That's where I found myself- at the lowest, southernmost minor league-Class D.

Sunny Florida.

The Florida State league hadn't been around as long as the Sally league, but I was ready for new blood. I tasted blood right away and got off on the wrong foot.

I still had the habit of daring any outfielder to throw me out trying to go from first to third on a single.

I'll never forget the day. It was May 11, our second wedding anniversary. Alex and I had planned on partying that night big time. While she didn't drink heavily like I did, she liked a glass of sweet cherry wine on special occasions. Her dad used to make that stuff and it brought family memories to her mind. We were locked in a game with the Red Sox farm team in Winter Haven. It was a scoreless battle going into the last inning.

The first man up for us was Jeff Grotenhuis, a slick-fielding second baseman who probably wouldn't make it to the big leagues because he couldn't hit a curve ball. But the Winter Haven pitcher didn't know that and he put the first pitch on a straight line on the outside corner. Jeff flipped his Louisville Slugger at the ball and knocked a Texas Leaguer into right field. Jeff wasn't very fast. This kid from a little town in Wisconsin called Cedar Grove had learned how to play baseball from his dad, Jerry, who had always dreamed of being a baseball player. But Jerry had to run his own father's farm and never got the chance. I always wondered how many fathers lived out their dreams in their sons.

Anyway, Grotenhuis was on first with no one out. Our manager had the next batter sacrifice the potential winning run to second. The next batter popped out. Guess who the next batter was?

You got it: Jock Moses. Being focused on the game like few players, I had watched the first pitch to Grotenhuis spin outside. I figured that's where the first pitch to me would head. I was a switch-hitter, batting right handed this time against the lefty on the mound. I edged closer to the plate and prepared to spank that baby to right field just like Jeff had.

The lefty turned his back to me as he wound up, whirled and delivered the fast ball on the outside corner. I swung. The ball was a blur to right field and so was I as I rounded first and headed for second. I had hit a lot of triples because of my speed. The ball I had just sent spinning down the right field line was one of those. At least that's what I figured.

I rounded second and forgot the baseball axiom of not making the first or third out at third. I had not noticed that Jeff had stumbled and fallen rounding third. I was too into myself. The third base coach had his hands up trying to put up the stop sign for me. I ignored the warning. The right fielder had a cannon for an arm and he rifled the ball from the corner near the wall to the third baseman on one bounce like Roberto Clemente of the Pittsburgh Pirates.

"Stop," yelled the third base coach. He had sent Jeff home, hoping he would score the winning run before I was nailed at third base. That hope never materialized. The third baseman was waiting for me and put the tag on my nose as I slid in head first. Since I was the third out and Jeff had not crossed home plate before they got me, his run did not count.

The result of my stupid move was threefold. Winter Haven did score in the bottom of the ninth to win, 1-0. Reminded me of my last stand with Custer when I was in fourth grade. The loss was the first result. The second was that I had a bloody nose. The third was unexpected.

Grotenhuis could have been upset with me like the manager was. The words the manager used to describe my play were ones we used to describe our enemy in Nam. But Jeff didn't say anything. He sat quietly on the worn-out and faded green bench in the locker room.

Finally I couldn't stand it. Everyone had filed out and had headed for the bus to take us back to Fort Lauderdale.

"Why weren't you upset?"

"You sure you want to know, Moses?"

"You bet. You could have scored the winning run and I screwed it up."

"That's true, Moses," he said as he put on his Cedar Grove High School baseball cap which I thought was a sign of immaturity. Your high school baseball cap? This kid was young, just out of high school.

"Why do you wear that stupid high school cap anyway?"

Jeff was not phased by my remark. "I don't think it's a stupid cap, Moses. It reminds me of my dad who never was able to see me play except for one game in high school. He had to plant the corn and beans and bring in the harvest. I hope some day that I can make the majors and I'll make a lot of money and I can give enough to my dad so he doesn't have to work anymore. Then he can watch me play and we can be together."

I felt sorry for my "stupid" remark.

"Sorry, G Man, I didn't know the cap meant that much to you. With that attitude of making it to the big time then, how come you weren't boiling after the game?"

"You sure you want to know, Moses?"

Same question. Twice.

"You bet."

"I have a real close family back in Wisconsin. My Aunt Bonnie is a Christian. She doesn't go around spouting Bible verses. She just lives her life the way a Christian should. I once asked her why she didn't seem too upset at life. The same question you asked me, twice. I don't tell anyone about my faith unless they ask, twice. The Bible says be ready to tell others but when they ask. I know you really want to know.

"Well, Aunt Bonnie said her faith was as small as a mustard seed. Not very big, but she felt it was enough because she didn't have to be big. God could. Maybe it's easy for a woman to be small in the world's eyes. Guys have this macho problem to be the big guy, the center of the universe, right?"

I nodded. Being small, I had always tried to act big.

"Bonnie told me that she had peace because her mind stayed on her Lord. Do you have that peace, Moses?"

I looked up at this tall, skinny kid who reminded me of Ichabod Crane from Washington Irving's short story.

I skirted the subject.

"Do I have peace, Jeff?"

112

He just stood there. I think he was waiting for me to answer my own question.

"Well, I think so," I finally stammered.

"You can know today, Moses. Do you believe in a Creator who made you?"

"Yea, doesn't everybody?"

I paused, then raced ahead like I had before on the bases.

"So, what are you getting at, Jeff?"

I was anxious to take my wife out for our anniversary. Party time.

"It's your wedding anniversary tonight, right, Moses?"

"You bet. How did you know?"

"I guessed. I saw that card in your locker addressed "To my wife."

"You're pretty smart."

He smiled. When he smiled it was like it was the sun coming up. Why was that I wondered.

"Can I see the card?"

"Sure."

"Wow," he broadened that smile as he read my words that I had composed rather than a card that Hallmark wrote.

"I didn't know you were a writer."

"Yea, I started in fourth grade. I did a little bit in college, too. I'd like to maybe do that for a living after baseball."

"You're a natural, Moses."

113

"Thanks, man."

"That's why you should have that peace, Moses."

"Waddya mean?"

"You can have that peace because you have certain abilities, like running the bases in baseball or writing cards to your wife."

"I still don't understand."

"Well, Moses, who do you think made you?"

"My pop and my mom." I hesitated. "And God, too."

He threw his duffle bag over his shoulder.

"Let's walk out to the bus. I bet everyone wonders where we are. And I know you're wanting to get back to Fort Lauderdale to party with your wife tonight."

How did he know that, I thought.

We would arrive back in Fort late because Winter Haven was in the middle of Florida and Fort was more than 200 miles south down the east coast.

All the lights were out as we walked up the damp ramp from the dressing room dungeon.

I shivered.

For just a moment I was scared. Jeff had struck with his caring arrows right in the heart. I had not been living an exemplary life. Despite being brought up in a home where you don't get drunk or fool around with women, I had wandered from the straight and narrow in the former case. In the latter matter, I had been tempted many times by some of the "baseball groupies" who tried to catch a well-molded athlete. Somehow, I escaped the young girls who set up the traps just like the fox in the children's story of "The Gingerbread Man."

I dismissed the pangs of conscience with the argument that I hadn't hurt anyone drinking and I hadn't been doing any womanizing.

I was hurtled back to reality.

As we walked side by side to the crest of the ramp, Jeff stopped and suddenly hit the light switch to the park lights. I felt blinded for just a minute.

"You know, Moses," said Jeff, "We all feel like we're in darkness at times, but then we see the light to the right way. That way, that truth, is Jesus Christ for me, Moses. He directs my paths. If I follow my Aunt Bonnie's advice by concentrating on him-you know like you concentrate when you're about to steal on the pitcher-I'll find the right path. With my mind on Christ -trusting him- I will find perfect peace." I looked up at Grotenhuis.

He had that peace.

For sure.

The peaceful night was shattered by the anger of one man- our manager of the Fort Lauderdale Yankees.

"I've been looking all over for you guys. If you expect you're going to keep an entire team waiting for you, guess again. This is gonna cost you. Both of you are fined $15 for the time we waited. Got that?"

Billy Golenbock was about my size, but scrawnier like a mouse who hadn't found enough cheese to fill out his bones. But his mouth roared every time he spoke.

When I look back on people who have affected my life, Billy G. was one of those guys; I knew he cared about all his players. He had been in the game forever; he had been fired from five different jobs as manager. But he didn't really have any trouble with his players, unless they gave up on him. Most of his problems lay with management. He was not a company man. He was a baseball man. He loved the Yankees.

"I'm still the best manager in baseball," Billy would tell us.

This 60-year-old firebrand then would scream, "I'm a proud Yankee. I'm a Yankee and I'll live or die like a Yankee."

Our proud Yankees manager wanted to leave Winter Haven just as much as I did. "You turn off the lights, Moses."

I flipped the cold gray metal handle down and the fluorescent bulbs full of light dimmed and went dark. I briefly thought about what Jeff had told me about the darkness we find ourselves in sometimes, but that later we see the light and find the peace.

Later, I thought.

Right then, I couldn't wait to return to Fort Lauderdale and to my honey's warmth. When I sat down on the cold, black vinyl a chill went up my spine. Reminded me of Minnesota mornings when you stepped outside and felt the blast of the crispness of the westerly winds that normally ripped across the state like the old-fashioned trains that scooted down the tracks.

Although the game had been lost, most guys were able to put the game behind them within a short period of time. I wasn't that way. I would replay the game play by play. I knew Billy did too.

Most of the guys were mentally drained and considering the long trip back most of them were asleep pretty quickly.

I had found a seat with Jeff right behind the manager up front.

Jeff was already gone to dreamland. Seemed like he was smiling.

Maybe Jeff would be a coach someday. He sure coached me "goodly." I looked back at all the guys. Friends were very important to me. I had always tried extra hard to make friends. Being the smallest kid in your class you have to find some way to stand up to be noticed. I had used my God-given talents (Were they really? Jeff would say so. My mom and pop would say so.) on the playground at Myles Standish Grade School and then at Folwell Junior High. I won my first letter at Folwell and my mom had put it in a scrapbook. That letter had been something to be proud of. Kinda like Billy G. was proud to be a Yankee.

In high school I captained the baseball team, but did not win the MVP award. I had wanted the award because I thought I was most valuable, but also because I needed the ego boost. Most kids look for that shot in the arm from their friends and since the players picked the MVP and not the coach I had sought that award. I should have been happy with the captain position, but that spot was chosen by our coach, Ron Blomberg, who had faced tragedy in his life when one of his sons died of leukemia and then later lost his wife to cancer, too. Blomberg reached past that pain. I saw his strength and wished I could siphon a little from him. I needed to accept what happened. Coach Ron Blomberg had.

As I looked back at the 25 guys on the team I realized we were a family. Of course, you are closer to some than others. At 27 I was older than most of the guys just like I had been in Nam. I knew I should be leading by example, but I wasn't sure that I was doing a very good job.

Even though I had been chosen to be captain of the baseball team in high school by my coach who saw leadership qualities in me, I had grown up as the youngest in my family where I had never been thrust in that position. So it was all a little foreign. Only Bill Kasch, Dennis Gust, and Brian Frank were close to my age. Kasch was a left handed pitcher with no fast ball but a big heart. Gust was his designated catcher, who couldn't hit and couldn't run, but he had a knack of stopping Kasch's best pitch, a knuckle ball that danced like a Hawaiian hula girl. If Kasch moved up, Gust would probably go with him. To be frank, Brian did not have much natural ability, but he wanted to learn. He did not have the knowledge of the game I did because I had played it from dawn to dusk when I was a kid. And I had watched every game on television I could and made mental note of what players did right. I liked the aggressive ones like Charley Hustle, alias Pete Rose of the Cincinnati Reds, but I would have been better listening to my manager, Billy Golenbock, who knew when to be aggressive and when not to. Discernment was Billy's middle name.

In the high-backed seat ahead of me, a flashlight was being feverishly handled by Billy G. as he raced over the box score and statistics for each pitch to see how we could have done better.

"Yes."

Billy's raspy voice confirmed he had found what he wanted. Suddenly he turned around, leaned over the edge of the seat and stared right at me.

Everyone in the bus was already asleep except for the manager and one lone player. How did he know I was awake? Did he know I burned with the same desire to win he did?

"OK, Moses, do you know the story in the Bible where your namesake puts out his hand and parts the Red Sea so his friends could escape the Egyptians?"

"Sure, skip. I went to Sunday School."

"Well, you're my oldest player and I need you-as a leader, I mean.

At times my manager would swear a blue streak to get a players attention. He also loved to party big time with his players at one bar after another. Now he was talking about the Bible? Now he wanted me to be a leader?

I didn't know if I could take all that in one night.

"What are you talking about, skip?"

"Your aggressiveness on the baseball field is what I love about you, Moses. You have that God-given ability to turn the game on its ear with that lightning you carry in your spikes. Your spirit carries to the other players, right?"

Before I could answer, the feisty coach with love and anger sputtering from him at one time or another, continued his onslaught. "Listen, Moses, the example you place before these young guys they will carry with them forever in the game. You are my spokesman."

"I can't be your spokesman."

"You know, Moses, your namesake in the good book said the same thing to his leader. Moses was able to change a stick into a serpent. You're like that- your hits snake through the infield like they have eyes. But when it comes to being a leader by talking to the players, you're not interested, huh?"

"Nope."

"OK. But do me a favor, remember that your actions have to do all your talking then. Was getting thrown out at third smart? Think about it. Well, I'm gonna get some shuteye."

I thought about it all the way to 2 a.m., which is when we arrived back home. All the other guys had cars waiting at the home field. I had something better. That is, someone better waiting for me.

Alex would always be there.

That's what a best friend does- be there for you in the darkness as well as the light.

She climbed out of her Volkswagen "bus" and flew to me as I stepped off the bus. Her long, slender arms wrapped around my stumpy neck. She squeezed gently.

I gave her some of her own medicine with a larger dose of squeeze.

"Ouch. Don't do that so hard."

Ever since returning from Nam I did everything hard.

One of my favorite singers had been Otis Redding, who had died in a plane crash in Madison, Wisconsin, right after I got back from Nam in 1967. One of his tunes was "Try a Little Tenderness." It was a theme I should have applied to Alex, but I hadn't figured that out yet.

"Let's go to Karter's Diner," she whispered in my ear.

"Why are you whispering?" I whispered back.

"Because, I don't want the other players to hear me. They might want to come along. I want you all to myself. It is our anniversary you know. Well, at least it was two hours ago."

Billy G. had skipped off the bus ahead of me.

He turned around to say good night.

"See you tomorrow, Moses. Be at the field at 4. Game's at 7. Don't stay out too late with that pretty lady. Don't forget what I said."

"O.K., skip, see ya tomorrow."

He slipped over the stones and headed for his old van. A couple of his coaches and Kasch and Gust tagged along. I knew where they were going. The Home Field bar normally closed at 2, but Billy and friends would greet the sun around 5.

CHAPTER 14

Another phone call of death

What did Billy mean about 'Don't forget what I said?'"

"Nothing, honey. He just thought I should be more of a leader on the field."

"Did something happen tonight that he would say that?"

"Well, kinda."

She looked at me with her big, soft blue eyes that made you think of a peaceful, blue lagoon. She brushed her long, silky black hair away from her eyes and waited for me to finish. She had a way of making me tell her things. Being the macho man, I wanted to make believe I could handle anything myself. I couldn't, but I wanted to make believe I could.

Of course, I caved in.

"We were tied in the last inning and Grotenhuis was ahead of me on the bases. He was about to score what would have been the potential winning run when I gambled and went for third base. They tagged me out at third before he scored and the run didn't count. And then the other team scored and we lost 1-0. Do you understand what I'm saying?"

"I heard the word 'gambled' and 'lost.' And I bet Billy doesn't like you gambling. I know neither of you like losing. Well, you haven't lost me. Let's go grab a couple of burgers and those wonderfully thick chocolate malts at Karter's." Just like that the hurt disappeared. I had Alex. That was all that counted at that moment. I didn't even fuss about going to Karter's. I had wanted to party at The Home Field. Alex must have guessed that.

While that night was pivotal for me as a baseball player because Alex reinforced what Billy had said about not gambling did hit home, there was another part of my life that did not change. My drinking continued. Kasch, Gust, Billy and I would often hit the taverns at The Home Field and even stop for more than a couple brews when we didn't take the bus. Since Billy had a van, anyone who wanted to go drinking could climb aboard and find some after hours fun. Of the towns we played in only West Palm Beach and Miami were close so those were the only away games where we took Billy's van. Fortunately for all of us, probably, because if all the games had been close we would have been in a summer-long drunk.

On the field, I turned soberly to the task.

I shifted gears and not only gunned around the bases with swiftness of feet, but also whipped around the sacks with swiftness of mind.

I did not make another out at third base all year running the bases.

My stolen bases skyrocketed to a personal best of 69 and I pumped my batting average to .320.

It was a great year. Billy G.'s managing skills, urging his players to go hard all the time, and his favorite play, the suicide squeeze bunt, jumped us into first place. We stayed there all year, winning the league championship by nine games.

The following year was even huger (That's bigger than huge, I believe.) than the previous one by a long shot.

But there were surprises.

A move to the Carolina league started things. I was back to Class B, two steps up from the Class D Florida State League.

The greatest thing about my career was that things were looking up- to the show, the major leagues. What made the season so memorable was not the action on the field, but off. And there were two reasons for those thrills.

The Yankees had decided to move me to Kinston in the Carolina League.

And Billy Golenbock moved with me.

Maybe the Yankee brass could see we were a team. If they thought that, they were right. We sprinted through the season just like the one before with my steals reaching an all-time high of 79, 10 more than 1970. The batting average zoomed 10 points higher. But before that happened we, Alex and I, found a Southern Baptist church with mostly black folks, who welcomed us.

Usually the start of the season was around June 1. That time of year in North Carolina is hotter than Mrs. Aaron's or Mrs. Moses' biscuits just out of the oven.

Pastor Calvin reminded me of Moses, the Biblical character. Not exactly like Charlton Heston in the movie, The Ten Commandments, with long wavy white hair, but he had a presence that said," Listen to me. I have something for you."

The church was called Greater Mt. Zion. The friendliness did not stop with the pastor. You couldn't even walk in the front door before someone would say, "Good mornin.'"

People actually came out of that church smilin,' the same way they went in. Some churches people go in frowning and leave the same way.

Why did they go anyway?

Didn't seem to change them.

I was happier than a Whippoorwill on a cool night that day. I thought I had everything going now. A great wife, a great baseball career, a great manager to help me move up to the major leagues.

But the drinking had not stopped.

In fact, it had intensified.

126

I started to do things that might stop my marriage and my career in its tracks.

One night Billy and I had grabbed a six pack at a little bar we had stopped at on the way home from a game.

That night I got sick before we made it home.

Billy had to stop his beat-up blue van to accommodate me.

My live-life-to-the-fullest manager dropped me off in the driveway at our home. It was the first home we'd had. Before in Greensboro and in Fort Lauderdale we had rented apartments. Now we had a white brick house, which we rented from a nice, older couple named Bob and Norma Tofall.

Billy leaned out the window and in a change of character, spoke softly, "You're a great kid, Moses. I've always thought you were a lot like me. That's why I was always so hard on you. I love you, brother."

Those words spilled out of Billy G. like maple syrup from one of those millions of trees in the Green Mountains of Vermont. They stuck hard and softly- in my heart.

All I could say was, "Thanks, Billy."

It was the first time I could remember that I had called him by his first name.

I was able to add, "Your confidence in me has gotten me to where I am today. See you tomorrow."

He smiled, touched the gold cross he always had around his neck and said, "I'm going home."

He backed the van out of the driveway, and sped off, rather recklessly, I thought.

As I stumbled rather recklessly in the back door, Alex greeted me with Joy in her arms.

"Hi, honey," I said with a heavy slur. "I'm home."

"Oh, Moses," she said.

She took Joy and put her down in her bed in our spacious three bedroom home. Alex was expecting our second child in a couple weeks.

I was left alone.

I sat down in an old, broken-down, light brown, leather chair. I suddenly felt a little bit like the chair. My head was a little broken down after drinking again, and my skin was already a light brown leather from the summer sun that beat on us at the diamonds where men played a boy's summer game.

I must have sat and thought about the universe and where I fit in it because it seemed like a long time before I was jarred loose from my thoughts. The phone must have been ringing for awhile because I didn't hear it. Alex had stumbled out of bed to answer the phone.

"It's for you, Jock," she said with a question on her face. "It's the police. What do they want?"

"I dunno." I took the phone. "Hello. What's wrong?"

The voice on the other end identified himself as a police officer in Prince William.

"Is this Jock Moses?"

"Yes," I said hesitantly. A fear swept over me like one of the cold waves that rolled in from the Atlantic Ocean, which was not that far away.

"You play baseball for the Yankees?"

"Yes."

"I'm afraid I have some bad news for you. Your Yankees manager, Billy Golenbock, was in a car accident tonight."

"What happened?"

"His blue van missed a curve. He must have been going too fast. The van ended up hitting the wall of an abandoned farm silo just off the road.Somehow I knew what the policeman's next words were going to be.

"Mr. Golenbock is dead."

The tears rolled continuously down my cheeks.

"I know this isn't the right time, Mr. Moses, but you were a real inspiration to the team and the fans tonight. I was at the game in an official capacity, of course. Could you call the other players?"

"Sure."

I hung up the phone and went in our bedroom to tell Alex. She had gone back to bed.

Suddenly I felt more alone than I had ever been. I had lost who I thought I was my inspiration-Billy. We were a team. But the officer had said I was an inspiration. As I climbed into bed I didn't feel like an inspiration to my wife, or my daughter, or to my second child, who I secretly hoped would be a son.

"Billy is gone, Alex."

"What do you mean?" she said half-awake, sitting up on her right elbow in the old, broken-down, second-hand furniture bargain she had found right before we bought our home.

"Billy was killed tonight in an accident. He was traveling too fast in his van and he missed a curve."

Alex was not someone who cried easily. She got misty eyed and squeezed me with one of her great hugs. "I'm so sorry for you, Jock."

She looked at me with her big blue eyes full of sorrow for me. "I know he was like a father to you."

"I'm going to call the other players to tell them the bad news. I promised the police officer I would. You know Alex now I know what drinking can lead to-death. I realize that I could end up like Billy. I know I could lose you and Joy forever. I'm not going to let that happen."

I didn't say the promise out loud, but silently I said, "I will never drink again."

CHAPTER 15

Storms after Billy's death

That season was dedicated to Billy. We all wore black arm bands as we tore up the Carolina League in towns like Frederick, Salem, Lynchburg, Kinston, Durham, Winston-Salem and Peninsula.

While I whipped through the Carolinas, leading the league in steals and finding my power stroke once more, Alex stayed home. The home runs were interspersed evenly that year, maybe because I was dedicated each night to "hit one for Billy." What I should've realized was that Billy would have wanted me to hit them for myself. However, I had one more little person to hit them for that year. Alex and I now had a son, Arnold, to go along with our delightful daughter Joy.

A father for the second time. Both kids had arrived on a nationally known holiday. Joy had come into our lives on Palm Sunday. That meant a lot to me since I had been born on Palm Sunday, too, a quarter of a century before. Now Arnold erupted into our lives on Father's Day. What a gift!

The promise?

I kept that no-drinking promise to myself even though Alex didn't pressure me at all to stop the trips to taverns after games. Because she did not nag me, I was more inclined to follow my own convictions. Since Vietnam if anyone in authority or someone I loved would make a suggestion I seemed to not only back away from the proposals but also to get my dukes up to fight.

The fight.

I wondered that summer- as I had more time to think since I was sober all the time - why I fought others.

Anger spilled out of me in gushes like an overburdened and weakened dike that would suddenly break. My anger was as much an irritant to others as a leaky roof is to a homeowner.

While the drinking had stopped completely, which I knew was vital if I was going to keep my woman and my two little kids, the deep-seeded anger had not only taken root but also had sprouted. Through the storms that erupted periodically throughout the year of Billy G.'s death, Alex remained calm. After one particularly tough loss (It was a good thing we won twice as many as we lost that year.) I came home in a bad mood. As I walked in the

132

door from a game where we had led by a big margin early and then lost our grasp on victory at the end to lose by one run, I lost my grasp on my emotions when I tripped on a tattered blonde doll named Mrs. Beasley that Joy dragged with her everywhere she went and then a yellow rubber bat I had given to Arnold on June 16, the day he was born.

"Alex," I screamed. "When are you going to have this house in order?"

One of the sounds which will always remain in my tattered mind is the yelling of boot camp drill instructors. While I never liked that sound, I accepted it as necessary. Now I was doing my best imitation of a Marine Corps DI. This time, it wasn't necessary.

"When I come home from the game tomorrow night, I want this house spit-shined, OK?"

Now I know when my DIs in San Diego-Bobby Bolton and Sgt. Scull (his real name)- in Platoon 3007 yelled I didn't smile. But when I fired out that angry salvo of words, Alex diffused my volley with a soft grin. "Sure, honey," she said. "I'll be glad to."

This left-handed woman not only cared for these two kids through a long day, but she carried wisdom too. Her riches and honor came from being a mother. Alex made those facts vividly clear the next day when I arrived home-from a win this time. When I walked through the door I was not thinking about a clean house. I was still back at my other home-the ballpark. That figured because I had been born in a ballpark.

My folks had come to this country for a visit right at the height of World War II. When they landed on the shores of New York and looked at the Statue of Liberty, I believe both of them realized this was where they wanted to be after suffering through war times in Europe. "That lady, she touched me," Pop told me once when I asked him about the first trip to the U.S.A. on one of our long walks on the sandy beaches of Spirit Lake on the outskirts of Sibley.

So, I guess I owe that lady a tip of the hat. I would have been a tuna fisherman like my father had been on the Isle of Man instead of a ballplayer. After getting off the boat after a month-long trek across the Atlantic Ocean, the first thing my pop wanted to do was do a little traveling. I remember my mom laughing about that. "I didn't want to go anywhere," my mom told me.

"But I would always defer to your father. I could see that light of excitement in his eyes and I did not want to hide that light under a bushel of tiredness that I was feeling. So we went, Jock. We took off for Vermont and that's where he saw all that green in the mountains.

"We came back to the east again. I could tell once we retraced our steps and came back through New Hampshire and then into Massachusetts that he wasn't happy. Kinda surprised me, too, because as we arrived on the ocean front I thought he would feel most at home there. Being a fisherman and all.

134

"But that was not the case. I believe he wanted a new adventure, Jock. I see that in you, too, son. You are a lot like your father." Strange my father didn't want to stay in Massachusetts because I was born in Fenway Park. My folks went to a game a week before I was expected.

Apparently I knew when I was home because I was delivered by a doctor in the visitor's dressing room. It figured the Red Sox played the Yankees that day. Destiny, right?

My father liked a clean house. And my mother would keep everything spic and span. Like my mother said, I was a lot like my father. So I was pleased to see a ship-shape house when I walked into our white brick home. I had stopped to pick up a rose from the bushes that lined the south side of the house. My little girl Joy would water them until a flood nearly ran down the driveway next to the house. I was happy at that moment and wanted to continue celebrating after a great night of scoring the winning run and stealing three bases. I thought I got a steal in this family. Why do I get mad at them? So, I picked a red rose and traipsed up the three steps to the back door.

"Hi Honey, I'm home" I said. "We won..."

Suddenly the play-by-play of my accomplishments for the night took a turn inside my mind to a back bedroom and I stood amazed at THE CLEAN HOUSE."Wow, what happened? A white tornado?" Alex was in the kitchen making butter horns for someone. My beautiful bride bent over backwards to please me. But then she treated a long list of people with love.

"Here, have one." This elegant lady with long black hair dappled with white specks of flour plopped a butter horn in my mouth.

"How was the game?"

"Forget the game. This place looks great. Thanks."

I turned to leave the kitchen, which was not like the kitchen my mother used to cook in Sibley, but this kitchen in Kinston had the same loving care. My wife and mother were alike in that characteristic.

Boom.

Alex hit me with a bombshell.

I had experienced exploding shells in Vietnam, but her next comments had the affect of one of those big mamas.

"Right after I started making these butterhorns after cleaning all day, Joy tugged at my apron that I was putting on. 'Mommy,' she said, 'when are you going to stop cleaning and be a Mommy again? Arnold is crying. He needs you...stop scrubbing.' Pretty good vocabulary for a two-year-old, eh? She went on.

'He needs you to stop scrubbing and pick him up and hold him. Would that be alright?'"

The last question Joy had picked up from me. I had learned that from Green Bay Packers coach Vince Lombardi. But that's another story. Suddenly I realized how off base I had been. I had been picked off base in the first inning after starting the game by walking. I had learned my lesson in the game because I watched the man on the mound more closely to pick up his move toward me. After that I stole those three bases. I had been off base with my family too. I needed to walk back in my mind and remember the lesson I had learned by watching for ways to move them. Then I could steal these three hearts away.

Alex had stopped me dead in my tracks.

I turned around.

She had picked up Arnold, who had been crying for his mother again. She cradled him as lovingly as the butter horn she had popped in my mouth a few moments before. Joy hung unto her apron, looking up at her mother, smiling, probably thinking, "Now you got it, Mom." Wish I had a camera to take a picture of this moment I thought at the time. However, that family photo will always be indelibly etched in my mind.

Something else happened that year that kept my life on a roller coaster.

Just like Nam was.

Up and down.

Life and death.

When I left for the far Asian shores around Thanksgiving of 1966 I left several precious items behind. At the time I probably did not realize as vividly as today what valuable assets I possessed.

Like...

- A pop who was proud of his son.
- A mom who protected me with her prayers.

- A fiance who not only loved me across the ocean but also kept my mom laughing with her phone calls from Chicago to Sibley.

Alex and I had known each other for more than a year, but since I was away playing baseball, we never had spent much time together. And when I flew to Southeast Asia the closest she could get to me was my family. So, she would call my mom to stop the crying. Maybe for herself, too.

CHAPTER 16

Back across the ocean

The crying was a way of life for the Vietnamese, who had faced death for centuries under Japanese and Chinese rule, then the French, and finally the fight for world supremacy between the two heavies in the world, the red, white and blue and the hammer and the sickle, who fought for the right to be No. 1.

The Vietnamese knew what No. 1 (you are the best) was and what No. 10 (you are the worst) was. I always wondered when the Vietnamese really meant it. You knew some of them wanted you there and some felt you were just another interloper in a steady stream of warmongers.

On the way to Vietnam in a giant bird that settled in Hawaii for 30 minutes the Marines hit the bars faster than they headed for the jungles and tunnels of Nam.

Mai Tai after Mai Tai went down the hatch. Getting drunk would stop you from hitting the wall of reality, wouldn't it?

Several hours later Okinawa came into view outside the green transport plane. Like Hawaii before, Okinawa looked like a temporary halt to what lay ahead. I put my hat back on as I rose to get off the plane. Did I really want to take the next step...to death?

Looking around at the young guys I realized we were in a heap of trouble. These guys couldn't even point out a dangling modifier in high school English let alone figure out how to communicate correctly in the bush. They all looked so young. That's because most of them were still teenagers.

But then I saw a line coming the other way. These Marines seemed to be the same age, but the look in their eyes was not the same. The wide-eyed look of the fear of the unknown which the incoming Marines possessed had been replaced by a distant and dastardly 100-yard stare of horror. Whether you were 18 or 23 like I was you saw and knew and felt the stare.

You knew you faced something or someone you couldn't beat. Marines are the best. That has been proven throughout history as President after President has had Marines storm the beaches to knock out the toughest foe.

But somehow before I went into my first operation in the jungle of Vietnam, I felt I couldn't win.

Americans don't lose, do they?

The end of the last sentence used to have an exclamation point, but a question mark had replaced my positive attitude after seeing the Marines who had stared this war in the face and marched past me like zombies. Foreboding feelings gripped me like an unfriendly relative. The feelings never left me.

Never!!!!!!!!!!!!!!!!!!!!!!

I tried to bury the uncomfortable nature that death slips over you like a burial shroud. Wasn't hard to find a graveyard to hide. I didn't know how long I would be in Okinawa but secretly I felt the longer the better. We were let loose in this country to go to the city to spend...our last dime? The girl at the bar thought so as she tried to ply away all the cash I had in one evening. The barbaric bar owners planned on the war interlopers paying for booze and sex. Get the guy drunk and take him to the back room. I looked in the future that night.

Trap.

Just like Nam.

I pretended to fall asleep to avoid the sex part after sending glass after glass of beer into my gurgling stomach that needed food not drink. Finally the girl left looking for another victim. There were many to choose from.

I arrived back in camp past curfew and I was afraid I would be slapped with time in the brig. Not all bad, I thought. At least I wouldn't be headed to unknown Nam. I would know where I was-behind bars. Safe.

"Don't worry," said the Corporal of the Guard as I waltzed in unsteadily like a duck in search of safety after being shot at by a bevy of hunters on Opening Day.

"You been humping, man. I'll cover your ass. Just be cool, OK? Get back to the barracks."

I had not been humping, but the Corporal showed he was semper fidelis (always faithful) to a fellow Marine. I crawled into the sack, Mac, and was asleep immediately. I had always been able to do that. My brother Garner used to get so mad at me when we were kids because he would be telling me about one of his exploits in sports or with girls and I would be snoring. He said first he would pinch my nose. When that didn't work, he slugged me in the stomach. Can you imagine a big brother doing that to a little brother? I can see the reverse of that scenario, but not the bully tactics. I guess I never could pick on anyone worse off than me.

That's why Aaron and I were close even though his family was richer monetarily than mine. The color black did not put him on top of the list as having it made in America. In fact, he was at the bottom.

When the next morning came with a bang the sky was still black and I felt like my spirit was at the bottom. There would be many more mornings like that- and nights, too.

All of us flying from Hawaii to Okinawa would have liked to have stayed there and not gone to Vietnam. But that was not our choice. We had to confront the yellow hordes, or as many called the enemy collectively Luke the Gook.

Luke wasn't around that morning. While I was surrounded with many other Marines headed for Vietnam, I felt alone. I did not know any of the guys around me. Unlike any other war the United States has been in before, in Vietnam you travelled to war alone. We came back alone, too, but I'm getting ahead of the   story.

We sauntered into another green monster and spiraled into the heavens. Funny, but I did not feel my feelings going up. Only my stomach. When we landed in Da Nang and the doors opened.

Oh, the heat.

I thought back to my Sunday school days back in Minnesota when my teacher, Mr. Nitz, taught us about Shadrach, Meshach, and Abednego who walked into the fiery furnace and were rescued by God without harm. Boy, did I feel like one of that trio. And, of course, just like all the Marines on either side of me, I wondered if I would be delivered.   Thirteen months lay ahead of me. It would mean I would miss two Thanksgivings and one Christmas with my family. While I was engaged to Alex I still would miss being with Mom and Pop and my brother and sister, too.

Every Christmas Pop would get out the family Bible which in many homes gathered dust and were often out for show. But in our home The Book was actually opened and

143

read from. Christmas Eve was something memorable. We would sit down to a meal of Swedish meatballs, lefse (a potato bread sliced thin which tasted great with butter, brown sugar-and cranberry sauce) and a rice pudding with an almond tossed in. Whoever found the almond would obtain a prize that my mom would buy. It was never an expensive gift but "the contest" to find the nut was a real battle.

I knew the battles I faced in the tour of duty would be hotly contested. But that Christmas in the sands off China Beach in Da Nang in Vietnam I hung on to the memory of my Pop reading the story of the birth of Jesus in Bethlehem.

The first month was not really memorable. It was almost like a war was not going on. We lived in huge tents-not quite as big as a circus tent that would be set up in small towns across America for the Ringling Bros. and Barnum & Bailey Circus, but about half the size. We had cots to sleep in, when we could sleep. While the war wasn't at our doorstep in the initial tour of duty during the steamy daytime, the lurking menace of death was above our heads at night. The line "the rockets red glare" in "The Star Spangled Banner" was a regular refrain that came into my head each night as the whoosh through the air permeated the night air. It was the second month when I met Mackenzie Aaron, Jr.

Even though everyone in Vietnam looked death in the face daily, even though the next step could be the last, there was not a constant thought about it.

Highlight of any day was mail call.

CHAPTER 17

Moses meets Aaron for the first time

From after Christmas in 1966 to the beginning of 1967 in Vietnam

Alex was never a writer. I had been one since writing that story in fourth grade about my hero Paul Giel, University of Minnesota Golden Gophers All American football player. My Mom had elevated the importance of the story by placing it carefully in a scrapbook. That act of kindness by my Mom impressed me in two ways. What I said about others was important. That was the first lesson-being careful about what I said. The second was that I had a talent in writing and I should never put myself or my abilities down. Of course, I forgot about both those lessons for a long time.

In the beginning of the tour of duty I wasn't sure if Vietnam was realistic. War time? We played football in the sands of our 1st battalion, 11th Marines base after Christmas and into January. Since most Marines are perceived as tough guys, we all had to act that part even if we weren't so tough. Football was part of that macho image. I had always loved baseball best, golf second and football next. But at that time football was king.

On January 15, 1967 the first Super Bowl game was played. Being a Minnesotan, it figured I would be a Minnesota Vikings fan. But when Vince Lombardi moved to Green Bay as head coach in 1959 and brought the Packers to prominence, to the top, I took the train ride of success with him. I became an avid Packers fan. Besides at the time there was no Minnesota Vikings team. The Vikings were not created until 1961. That green-and-gold (the colors of the Green Bay Packers) support was what started the friendship I had with Aaron.

We had just received the mail and we were all devouring each word like a pack of wolves devouring a wounded caribou. "Great," I yelled.

I must have shaken the guy's tree next to me because this guy was as tall as a 150-year-old oak tree. Or at least that's the way it seemed to me.

"Heh, man, don't blast my ears out."

I smiled. "Sorry, but my girl friend just told me the Packers won the Super Bowl." I had a Wisconsin cut-off sweatshirt on. Macho again.

"Are you from Wisconsin?"

"I'm from Minnesota, but the Packers have been my favorite team since 1959 when Lombardi came."

"I have relatives in Wisconsin so that's how I started following them. Down south in Georgia where I'm from there aren't any pro teams."

"Do you think you guys will ever have pro football?"

"Think about it. We just got the Braves from Milwaukee this year, so I don't see why we wouldn't get the Packers from Wisconsin soon."

"Are you kidding? They'll never..."

This giant was holding his sides laughing.

"You were fooling, eh? You got me. What's your name?"

"Mackenzie Aaron, Jr."

When he said his name he stated it with a sense of family pride because he accentuated the junior, which I thought he meant he was proud to have his father's name. Some "juniors" would not have liked their father's name.

"What's yours, man?"

"Mine? Moses is my name and fighting is my game."

Aaron looked down at me and started laughing again. He had a sense of superiority about him that gave me mixed feelings. Unlike a lot of black dudes I had met in the Marines, he did not give you the feeling that just because you were white and he was black that he was inferior. He stood his ground, not just physically but mentally. His intellect tried to dominate you. Although that was the part I

148

did not like initially, I learned that it was a game with him. He knew he could swipe you away with one swing of his huge arm, but he did not want to take advantage of you physically because that would be unfair. He would rather spar with your brain.

"Moses, huh?"

"Do you realize, Moses, that we are brothers?"

He gave me that glare that I learned to decipher through the next year. Aaron had come over just before I had and he would leave before I would by about a week.

"What are you talking about?"

"Ever read the Good Book?"

"The Bible?"

"No, Playboy!"

"Playboy?"

"Oh, man, you are something else!"

His face got all contorted and he roared with laughter for the third time in the 10 minutes since we met.

"Listen," Aaron said in his didactic way, which I also learned to appreciate because I also talked in a teacher's tone, "there were these two guys named Moses and Aaron in the Bible. Moses was the leader of the Israelites. God told him to tell the people that He would let the people out of the bondage they were suffering under in Egypt. But Moses said he was not accustomed to public speaking. Moses told God to send someone else, so God relented and said, OK, your brother Aaron can tell them. Wonder if that's the way we'll be. I mean, like brothers."

149

He looked at me with that stare that bore right through me. His eyes did not have any merriment in them. This time he was asking a serious question.

"Brothers, huh?"

"Yea, think so?

I couldn't let this guy get the best of me, I thought. An idea popped into my head.

"Listen, man," I said. "There is no way we can ever be brothers. I mean, you're black and I'm white. That difference separates us. So, just forget it."

I gave him my best larrupin' Leatherneck look.

He looked quizzically back at me.

"Do you really believe that? What kind of education you got, brother?"

"I graduated from the University of Minnesota, brother," I shot back.

"Well, if you're so smart, brother, then how come you think color is what counts most?"

"Cuz that's what people see first, don't they?"

"Maybe some," this big Mac said, stroking his little goatee as he tried to figure me out. "Well, my mama always told me we were all related back to Adam and Eve so that makes us all brothers. You really are prejudiced, aren't you?"

"You bet. I think you tall people over 6 feet are trying to put us small people 6 foot under."

I couldn't hold my ruse any longer.

The laughter bubbled out of me like a bad chemistry experiment.

"Man," Aaron said, "you were checking me out for my true feelings, right? I was trying to do the same thing to see if you were an all right dude. Since we were both doing the same thing, blue-eyed soul brother, we better keep this language battle on the same wave length. I will be calling in artillery for you when you go out in the field. That's where you're going aren't you?"

"Not just yet. I want to play some football on this white sand like Max McGee did for the Green Bay Packers in the Super Bowl game. The story my girl sent me said McGee had only caught four passes all year before the Super Bowl. Since he didn't expect to play he was out all night drinking and carousing with a woman. So what happens? He gets called by Lombardi to go in the game and he ends up grabbing seven balls and scores two touchdowns and is the hero of the first Super Bowl."

We knuckled down to some hard-nosed tackle football. There were no Super Bowl rings to play for but just a bunch of guys trying to forget the war around them. There were other ways to forget.

I cried out after one exhausting dash, "It's party time."

"I'm right behind you, Moses. Race you to the beer tent."

Races I loved. Speed was something I had possessed since I was seven years old and an older girl named Judy used to chase me home.   While Aaron could haul his massive body pretty good, he couldn't catch the granny.

"Granny" had become my nickname when a friend of mine named Jay Welcher started a radio show and asked me to add my talents to the all night conversation we used to keep everybody sharp. No Lieutenant Colonel had come up with Welcher's idea to keep everybody awake and alert. Welcher was only a corporal like me, but he was smart. He wanted to stay alive.

So did I.

I joined his radio show.

"Granny" came from one of comedian Jonathan Winter's made-up characters, Grandma Frickert, who used to talk like this: "Hey, sonny, did I ever tell you about my brother, Lamar Gene Gumbody? He's a strange fellah. Wasn't very smart, kinda like Gunny Denny. We used to keep him cutting grass a lot. Bet Gunny Denny would cut the grass right here in all this sand if you gave him a lawnmower. Where's the grass, sonny?"

The grass was what other guys used to forget the wings of war that carried them into nothing but death, whether it was their side or our side.   Marijuana came from the villagers as easy as the Tiger-piss beer we pirated from them. Pot was not the port I headed for on my forgetfulness ship. Except for one time. A time that could have been costly-and deadly.   Every night the Marines at the headquarters battery, 1st battalion, 11th Marines would go out on a listening post (LP). One night I went out with Ed Mitschke, a tall Texan. (Yes, all Texans are tall.)

Before I made the trip 200 yards in front of the barbed wire that surrounded our position, I took a trip on pot for the first time. A couple guys figured I should try it. Being stupid, I listened. After only two joints, I was flying. That's how I hit the L.P.-on a high.

"O.K. Mitschke, I'm in charge," I slurred to the tall Texan. "I'll go way out there with my slick handy dandy radio and you stay back here where ol' Luke the Gook can't see you. You're too tall to be out there anyway." Mitschke probably should have tied me up right there like a good Texan corrals a young bull calf and gone out himself but he didn't. He may not have known what condition I was in.

"You stay here." I pointed to a place behind a sand dune that about half covered up this giant. Sometimes I felt like I was in the Land of Giants. Aaron was 6-foot-6 and Mitschke was approaching that mountainous plateau.

"O.K. Granny," he said slower than molasses dripping out of a maple tree in Vermont in the dead of winter.

While Mitschke was less than 100 yards outside the concertina barbed wire of our base where around 100 guys slept and 18 kept watch from the six sand bunkers that were placed strategically in a circle around the outer perimeter, I stretched myself to about 200 yards out.

On the east side of the base there was a road that meandered up and down Highway One, which ran from between Chu Lai and Da Nang where we were located and Hue, the imperial capital of South Vietnam, to the north. While we protected our position around the entire base, normally the two guys on L.P. would head out southwest and northwest of our base position.

The "highway" that ran east of our position was only an Arnie Palmer drive away from the China Sea. So we figured most of the danger lay to the west, into the jungle where we waited for the enemy. You could never say all the danger lay in one direction in Vietnam. The war was fought in one yard block areas, where land mines bounced up from hell and exploded or a hand grenade suddenly dropped down ready to send a buddy heavenward. That night on the listening post was a memorable one. From 2300 to 0300 (that's 11 at night to 3 in the morning.) a tall Texan and a minute Minnesotan were like scouts hunting for Indians in the old West.

Fortunately it was a memorable night because nothing happened. Why was that memorable? Don't forget I was high on pot. After the four-hour shift was over, I crawled the 200 yards back, thinking I was a big man for going farther than this giant buddy of mine.

I mumbled to Mitschke. "Well, we scared 'em tonight, big guy. They must have known better than to fool with us United States Marines."

He smiled. "Why did you go out so far, Granny? That was past where you were supposed to be."

"I wanted to get close to Luke the Gook. I wanted to show 'em."

"You got to be careful, Granny," Big Ed said seriously. But he got over that mood. He quickly changed back to his happy self. "You know, you still got the 'Granny Show' to do when you're Corporal of the Guard. We couldn't get along without that."

I appreciated Ed. He would never rip you like most of the guys, even though they all did the slamming in good-natured fun. He was just one of those rare nice guys you meet once in awhile.

Be careful he had said.

That statement did not hit home until the following day after I had slept through breakfast, which I was allowed to do after being on L.P. When I woke up no one was around. Two of my best friends, Troll and Mouse, had headed for breakfast. Troll was so ugly he looked like he belonged under a bridge we used to say. Besides, that's where trolls lived in fantasy books. This Portuguese kid David Marks from Santa Ana, California, was short and stocky. Mouse, a Mexican kid Robert Hernandez from the state of Washington, was just short. He used to get tortillas and enchiladas from his sister to fatten him up because his family figured he was living on rice. Even though he wasn't living on rice, Mouse never grew.

That was O.K. We liked Mouse the way he was.

Troll, Mouse and I and other NCOs (Non-Commissioned Officers) lived in the same tent on base. It

155

was like a circus tent. War could not be compared to circus fun, but there were elements of each that were similar. Animals galore paraded around the war just like the elephants and the lions and the tigers that strutted their stuff inside the ring.

We had our animals, too. First and foremost the guy who stood out in the wild animal category was Sheridan, an Irishman, who we called "The Wild Man." He actually kept statistics on kills. Sloan was another guy who was a terror, a warrior through and through out in the field. However, when he came back from the field, he was transformed into a regular human being. Sloan was a basketball player who had a promising career ahead of himself in the pros if he ever got home to the States. He was a tremendous defender in basketball I had read in a newspaper clipping he carried around in his billfold. He didn't carry around the clip because he wanted to brag, but he said he wanted to remember home; he wanted to focus on the life he had ahead. That's why he was such a mean dude.He was determined to stay alive.

Then there was Donovan, another warrior, but he didn't care if he stayed alive.

"Granny," he told me in an interview I was doing for the Marine publication, the Sea Tiger, and maybe it would be printed in Stars and Stripes, which was the newspaper for all services," I don't care if I die here or at home.

"Back home I live in a town called Watts in California where life is so bad that the rats eat better than us dark folks. So, I'm mean because there's nothing to look forward to. Who was ever nice to me?" The United States government? Hardly. A larger percentage of blacks went to jail for various crimes than whites. About 48 percent of guys in prison back home were black. And blacks only made up around 12 percent of the population. One conclusion to that formula of four times too many blacks end up in prison could be that the life the blacks have been given isn't enough so they have to steal and kill to make it fair.

Many were thrown in the Marines just to alleviate crowded jails in the U.S. So, the "cream of the crop" was sent to Southeast Asia or at least many who didn't care about living in hell in the U.S. were fired 10,000 miles across the ocean like a silver shell ready to explode. Donovan was like that.

Set to explode!

Probably the best Marine I ever met was the Duke of Earl. He was a leader not only for the blacks, but also for the whites. He led by example not by giving you a lecture on the way to handle the daily problems of the war.

If Earl had grown up in Africa he would have been a chief. But Earl Nobleman was appropriately named, because he truly was a noble character. Maybe that's why he deserved to be called the Duke of Earl. Of course, a song about that time with the title "the Duke of Earl," came out and many of the soul brothers-and it didn't matter whether you were brown-eyed or blue-eyed - used to harmonize that song when we were around Nobleman. He would just smile, raise his huge hands, which were bigger than a couple of hams, shake his head, and walk away without saying a word.

He was smart, a man who knew what he was doing but didn't smart off about the fact that he had it all together.

"Watch what I do and follow," was the message.

"Whenever the Duke of Earl is in the middle of the attack from Charlie (aka the Viet Cong)," said Donovan, "I want to be next to him. I know I'll be O.K."

Later, being next to the Duke of Earl turned out to be a false sense of security for Troll.

Security was always key for all of us. Like the night I had been on L.P. The reason I was there was to make sure we were all secure and safe. But I had taken a giant step towards throwing away that security blanket by smoking pot just before going on watch.

And while it did not sink in while I was out on watch, when I woke up alone the next morning, for a fleeting moment I was scared. I never liked being alone. I was a gregarious person. I knew I would marry Alex when I left the Marines and we would have a bunch of kids.

I sat upright in the cot.

"My God," I said in a direct comment to the Creator like he was sitting in the tent with me. "If the VC had ripped past me when I was high, they could have killed my buddies. I would have been guilty of murder."

That was the first time I smoked pot-and the last. Shame swept over me like an avalanche of hot lava that burned my psyche if not my body.

CHAPTER 18

Doing the right thing

Although I wanted to write Alex and tell her what just happened, instead I wrote to tell her I wanted to make love with her the moment I got off the plane.   And we could start having kids immediately.

Being a moral guy was important to me. It was also vital to my bonnie lass, Alex. She knew I loved her for more than her body, even though she was so skinny she had to run around the shower to get wet.

So, how did she take this supposed reversal in morals?

To her credit, not seriously. Being apart does strange things to people.   Absence makes the heart grow fonder somebody once said. Not seeing each other for an extended period can also make you dream up all sorts of possibilities-unless your relationship is solid. Then you can say all sorts of things and your "mate" has the capability of sorting out the truth. Dreaming about Alexandra became an obsession in Nam for me. I had been engaged to a girl in college, but she didn't want to be the wife of a baseball player. She wanted a 9 to 5 guy. Not me. So, not us. I took the ring back.

Which led to a hairy happening between me and this girl Janie. We had been engaged since we were sophomores. When it came around to the end of our senior year, apparently this doll wanted to make sure I knew who was the boss.

"I can't be the wife of a baseball player," she whined. "I want you home at night. I'll be lonely."

"For what?"

"For you, of course. What else?"

"Well, I think all you care about is my body. You've been trying to get me to go to bed with you ever since you started hanging around the wrong crowd. You know I can't do that."

"Oh, Jock, I need you," as she draped her claws around my neck.

"Janie, are you telling me that if I follow my abilities in baseball, you can't be part of my dreams?"

"Can't you do something else? You wrote for the school paper. You could do that."

"Someday, maybe. For now, I have to follow that dream."

"I can't do that."

"Give me the ring then."

The ring came off so quickly it was if she was looking for a reason to separate us.

"Here then." She handed it to me, twirled like a majorette, and spun off.

A couple weeks later I received a phone call at my dorm.

"Jock," a soft voice whispered.

"Janie?"

"Jock, I can't stand it without you. Please come over to my dorm."

"We're through, Janie."

While I said those words, I stumbled on them because I loved her. But I knew, too, I had to follow the path that was best for me. Otherwise I wouldn't be true to myself, the person my Creator had molded.

"If you don't come over, I'll..."

"You'll what Janie?"

"If you don't come over," she repeated the words like they were lines from a play that she had been rehearsing. She finished the sentence," and take me to a motel, I...I am going to kill myself."

Some may have not taken that line seriously. I did. She suddenly became irrational.

"I'll slit my wrists and kill myself if you don't take me to a motel."

"O.K., Janie. I'll be right over."

I ran over the mile to her dorm in probably record time, racking my brain to figure out what I was going to do. Janie had some of the answers. "We could go to Faribault on the bus and stay at a motel or hotel there," she said, suddenly rational because I had rolled over to her desires.

"Fine," I said, but it was not fine. Not at all.

While many guys would have jumped into bed with this doll, who later became a United Airlines stewardess, I did not always focus on self gratification, which I thought she did.

When we got to the little town south of the Twin Cities, we found an old hotel and I registered under "John Smith," not telling them I had someone with me. I hated lying. I hated being there. But what if Janie had meant what she said about killing herself. I would have been responsible for her death just like I would have been responsible for the death of my buddies when I was high on pot while I was on L.P.

I met her in the dark, dingy hallway and we snuck up the steps to a fourth floor room. The room was done in dirt and dust with an old bed in the center- the center of our problems I thought.

Somehow, I found I was given some extra courage to not do it that night. The next morning we jumped on the bus like a couple of frogs on a lily pad and after arriving back on campus we drifted our separate ways. She found her self gratification in one of the guys in her new-found crowd.

While I was angry then, I was glad later that she was not the one to share my dreams. Now, Alexandra is someone every guy would be proud to call "wife." My buddies would add little notes on my letters saying they "wanted her bod" and Alex probably dismissed the messages of those of crazed Marines more than 10,000 miles away.

Before I could finish the letter, though, that I was writing to Alex the night after I had been high on watch, Troll and Mouse roared back into the tent and harassed me about being an old Granny sleeping through breakfast.

"Man, I don't know anybody who would miss hot cakes and coffee, you ol' lady who needs that mud juice (which was what we called Marine coffee) to get jump started in the morning. I mean it is time to get up, isn't it Granny?"

That was Mouse in his favorite Mouse That Roared impression.

"And listen, Granny," added Troll, "you are going to need a lots of grub to stay strong for our Operation Stone. We leave tomorrow."

That was Troll, telling you stuff that you already knew.

That foreboding feeling came back to the front of my mind. That feeling that had taken a temporary vacation zapped me. I shuttered. "No problem, Troll. With you leading the pack Charlie will run away screaming. "Number Ten face."

Number Ten, of course, meant his face was the worst looking.

Troll threw back his walnut-shaped head and laughed.

"O.K., Granny, I'll be the point to protect your face. Heh, who you writing to? Your girl?"

Before I could answer this portly, gregarious Portuguese, he was off and running at the mouth again. "I can't wait until mail call today. Today could be the day."

We all knew what Troll meant. He had gotten his wife pregnant before he left for Vietnam and she was due any day.

"I bet it'll be a troll instead of a boy or girl," I shot at him.

"By the time I get to see my kid I'll be as old as you, Granny," he fired back.

Mail call came with the news we had hoped for. Troll was a daddy. He and his wife Shirley had a new baby girl named Jolene. We celebrated big time. A case of beer and two fifths of rum that Matty Bryk had secured from someone in a deal. Bryk had just received a "Dear John" letter telling him he was no longer the john in his girl's life. So he was drowning his sorrows while Troll, Mouse and I drowned in joy.

I had to carry Mouse to the Corporal of the Guard bunker that night and stand his watch because he was in no shape to stand anyplace. He was so small he got drunk faster than the rest of us.

Morning came too fast.

We had breakfast-hot, steaming coffee, which made us all wide-awake drunks. And we scarfed down ham and

165

eggs and a bunch of bananas, which were prevalent in Vietnam. Our new commanding officer was Paul Skibsrud, who I had dubbed, "Skibby." He didn't seem to mind the nickname instead of the normal "Captain." He was my age-nearly 24- so I guess he felt we were equal.

Equal? Funny word in the United States Constitution. Did the black man, the Mexican, the Jew get the same treatment as the white man under the law of our land?

Actually no one is equal. We are fearfully and wonderfully made as an inspired writer once put it. Even "identical" twins have different fingerprints. Mr. Behnke, a science teacher I had in high school, taught me that.

CHAPTER 19

A decision from a lieutenant goes all wrong

The lesson I was to learn that hot boiling day was one I would have liked to have skipped. The whole classroom in Vietnam reeked of one big lesson on how not to solve a problem. When we came to that country, we did not know that.After this one day, I knew we didn't belong there.

Lt. Hardie wasn't with us that day in Vietnam. He had been sent to Japan on official business and we didn't know how long he'd be gone. A rookie "looey" by the name of Brock was to lead us on Operation Stone. We had been encased in a safety cocoon of concertina or barbed wire that supposedly protected us from harm. Now we were going through the gates-not of hell, but maybe to hell.

The gates were swung wide open like the jaws of Moby Dick, Herman Melville's Great White Whale, and we walked slowly through them, not sure of what lay ahead. One guy did not have that foreboding feeling, though. Since Troll was a brand new papa he was like a kid on the night before Christmas with visions of sugarplums dancing in his head.

He raced right through the jaws.

New lieutenants like to show they're in charge right away. Lt. Hardie wasn't that way, but he wasn't a new lieutenant. He had come through the ranks before becoming an officer. He was one of us. Like a never-used handkerchief in the pocket of a suit, Lt. Brock pretended he had plenty of experience when he had none.

"O.K.," he said in a fake gruff voice," if you're in such a hurry to search and destroy those gooks, you take the point."

He pointed at Troll, not even knowing who Troll was or if he was qualified. Troll was not qualified, but Brock did not know that. Lt. Brock stood there with his arms crossed, in his fresh, pressed fatigues that looked like he was going to be in a parade at Quantico, Virginia, where the brass trains officers. He put on his stern look, scowled and then, showing his ineptness, said, "What's your name? What's your rank?" The looey had already told Troll to lead us without investigating his "point man." The crazy question was that he asked him what his rank was.

All Brock had to do was open his eyes and look closely enough to see Troll was a lance corporal.

What this rookie looey had was no cognizance of his surroundings and what he had did not include leadership. He did receive awareness of his environment that day, but leadership is not something you acquire. You either got it or you don't.

The dusty road threw up smoke signals as our rice paddy stomping boots shuffled out of the base camp, where we felt safe, and into never-never land, where we didn't. The smoke signals probably carried a message for this long line of Marines that stretched out like a king cobra, which is the longest poisonous snake known. Whether we would deliver the poison or be snake-bit ourselves lay ahead.

The squad of 10 guys ahead of me wound its way down the narrow pathways that separated the rice paddies that were chiseled into the Vietnamese terrain like a giant patchwork quilt with perfect squares. This day was not perfect. It was boiling even though we had started early at around 7 in the morning. The sun had only started its ascent on the mountain of heat, but its effect on us was startlingly substantial.

The Duke of Earl was not influenced, but the little guys like Mouse and Russell, Silva's pride and joy from rural Georgia, were hardest hit.

The little guys didn't complain. Marines don't have the word "complain" in their vocabulary if they were tough enough, which was most of the time. But sometimes the bitching would creep out like an unwanted oil spill.

This was one of those days.

Sheridan, the wild man, was ready for action. He had already been in Nam for too long. This was his second tour of duty. He had gone home for 30 days and come back for another stretch. He wanted to put more notches on his kill list.

"I don't have enough slits on this belt of mine," said Sheridan, who was in an uglier mood than usual. "I"ll rip open those slant-eyed bxxxxxxx.

Donovan and Sloan, who had plenty of experience, too, were the warriors you could count on through the thickest "stuff." I had heard from other guys who were combat reporters that they were the best one-two punch when it came to reacting to any surprise attacks, which was the way the Viet Cong fought the whole war.

That day I was the combat reporter, assigned to cover the action in Operation Stone, my first. I didn't know it at the time, but there would be 27 more operations I would cover. This one, though, would always be the toughest to remember.

I didn't know that the story of this operation would be hard to write, but one of the other guys had a premonition.

His name was Ford, and he was from Detroit, Michigan.

Like the cars in Detroit, Ford was a productive and practical machine. He was a genius when it came to strategy in the field. Donovan and Sloan depended on Ford. So did the Duke of Earl.

"Listen to Ford," said the Duke as we headed out the gate. "The Lieutenant may be giving orders, but Ford will know what to do. I have been in this country now for 10 months. My last 90 days I want to stay close to Ford. Listen, Granny, this guy is a prophet. He knows what's going to happen before it happens."

"Sure," I said with disdain for anything that resembled some kind of superstition or voodoo quality.

"Just pay attention," finished the Duke of Earl, who was built like a bowling ball, as he almost knocked over the entire squad like bowling pins. "Listen, you guys," his voice booming out of the ebony face that stood out on this bright day, as his attention turned to Marine business instead of voodoo superstitions, "spread out. This is your first time for some of you guys. If you're close together one bouncing betty is going to wreak havoc with more than one at a time."

A "bouncing betty" was a homemade explosive that lay beneath the surface. If you tripped a wire along the path, the mine would bounce up and rip your private parts away, making you just like a "betty." The VC didn't have to kill you, just put you out of commission and back to the states, where they thought you belonged.

I wondered if the South Vietnamese thought we should go back to the states where we belonged. No one had really gone out of their way to be nice to us since we'd been in camp. Sure, there were the locals who were trafficking some illegal device or another-mostly marijuana-but I never felt like the red carpet had been rolled out when I arrived.

The Duke of Earl was a sergeant to end all sergeants. My new found friend Aaron was a sergeant, too. While Aaron did not go out in the field, and that left him somewhat detached, he still had a nasty job in the war. He called in artillery for sergeants like the Duke, who knew what was happening in the bush. Aaron was handed a blueprint to fire at targets, but he never saw the results of his decisions. Sometimes the decisions led to death. Maybe that's what finally snookered him when he went back to the States. He never saw his destruction.

Others did, however.

Lt. Brock did not rely on the savvy of the veteran black man, Sgt. Earl Nobleman. Rather, he wanted to show that all educated white guys would always be superior to uneducated black guys. The education of the Duke was something else he didn't know about. If he listened to the Duke with his phrase "wreak havoc" Lt. Brock might have guessed this was a man with a strong vocabulary, one who probably went beyond high school.

In fact, the Duke had graduated from Winston-Salem State in North Carolina where he starred in flipping metaphors in English class as well as behind-the-back passes on the basketball floor. He said he had two goals. One was to become a star in the pros and the second was to use the stardom to write a book about his life to inspire young kids to rise above the low expectations that white America had for young black kids.

Not only did Lt. Brock have low expectations for young blacks, but older ones like the grizzled-face Duke of Earl.

"Listen, Sergeant, I'm in charge here," Lt. Brock started, making his first mistake. Everyone respected the noble Duke. Not just the blacks, like Donovan or Russell, but the whites, like wild man Sheridan and the prophet Ford.

Before the Duke could speak, Lt. Brock rattled out orders. "O.K. Lance Corporal (Brock had finally figured out the rank for Troll but he still didn't know his name was Marks.), you listen to me now." This seriocomic figure looked at the rumpled papers he held in his hands.

"We're heading due west to checkpoint Albert. I'll let you know how far it is."

"Letting the men knew how far we're going today would help us all pace ourselves, sir," said the Duke.

The lieutenant lashed out at the Duke like a mongoose snatches a snake."Listen, sergeant, I will let you know what you need to know when you need to know it, is that clear?"

"Begging your pardon, sir, but Lt. Hardie always did it that way," said the noble leader with plenty of respect. But apparently the respectful tone did not win over the new lieutenant.

"Well, today," he blustered, his face turning as red as blood spurting out of a wound, "we're doing it my way."

Brock turned quickly, nearly falling.

The Duke stood there dumbfounded, not believing what he was hearing. I had only known Duke for a short time, 90 days, which was exactly what he had left in country. But I knew his record because I was privy to the records of all the guys in our base camp and those who were supported by the artillery unit. Duke's record was not clean. He had been busted from Sergeant to Private once for disobeying a direct order to not advance into a tree line where Viet Cong were suspected to be. He did, knocking out a sniper who had been picking off his fellow Marines one by one. There were no other VC there, only one. Instead of being given a medal, he was busted for disobeying an order. Unfair? War wasn't fair. The politicians stayed in their white houses or palaces while the poor peons and peasants killed each other. No, it wasn't fair, but that didn't stop the Duke of Earl from doing what he had to do, the right thing.

I thought the Duke, who had worked himself up to Sergeant again with bravery that got him promoted rather than demoted, was about to head the other way in rank again. He looked like he was about to explode.

"Duke," I said. "Come here a second, will ya? I got a question on something."

I didn't really have a question, but I needed to diffuse the bomb about to go off.

174

"O.K. Granny," Duke said, looking at the spinning Lt. Brock as he stumbled down the trail. "What do you need?"

"I'd like to do a story on just one guy on this first day of Operation Stone. You have been on so many. Any suggestions on how to go about it? I mean, who should I pick?"

He took one more glance at Brock. "Shit. That man not only stumbles in his brain, but he can't walk either."

I'd never heard the Duke swear before. He was cool when it came to the right words. He must have been near the boiling point. I was glad I distracted him.

The calm and cool Marine came back quickly as he turned to me. "Maybe you want to take one of your buddies, like you, on his first operation. That word 'first' always seems to crop up in newspapers. How about LCpl. Marks? What do you call him? 'Troll?' Take him. Scoot up there with him. Follow his every step as point man. That's the toughest spot for anybody.

"And Brock thinks a new guy should be there. Man, he's crazy. I wish Lt. Hardie was here today. I'm going to talk to Ford to see what he believes is going to happen today."

I had been at the back of the pack, but I sprinted up to be with Troll. He was about as far as it was from the pitcher's mound to home plate, which was 60 feet, six inches.

As I passed Lt. Brock, I nearly knocked him off the narrow trail which was not any wider than home plate, which was only 17 inches across. Funny how I related distances and measurements to baseball. I knew why. I wanted to be back home. And here I was only on my first operation. I didn't know how many I would go on. One thing I did know. This could be my last. It could be anyone's last.

"I'll be up with LCpl. Marks, Lt. Brock. Sgt. Nobleman said it would be all right."

I could tell Brock didn't like the press tagging along, but I knew he felt stronger about me following orders from a sergeant rather than a lieutenant. He scowled, but didn't say anything.

Since the trail was so narrow between the rice paddies, it was hard not to look down all the time. It was wise to check for any trip wires, of course. The next step could be your last.

When I reached Troll up front, I stopped him to tell him what I was going to do. "You're going to be the star of a feature story about a new guy on his first patrol on his first operation. And to be put at the point right away...well, that's unheard of says the Duke of Earl."

"Aw, go on, Granny, you're going to write a story about me? My little girl will love this when she's old enough to read, that is. I can't wait to hold her in my arms."

I looked back at the squad. Right behind us were Donovan and Sloan, the two mature warriors. I felt safer with those two guys along. Behind them, though, was wild-man Sheridan. With his red hair and handle-bar mustache he reminded me of the cartoon character Yosemite Sam, who always seemed to have his two six guns blazing. Then came the other red-haired Marine, Russell. Two guys with red hair. One guy white. One guy black. Brothers of the red hair, I chuckled to myself. Mouse, Mitschke, Lt. Brock, Ford and the Duke of Earl completed the squad.

There was a distinct separation between Lt. Brock and Ford and the Duke of Earl. The Duke of Earl had pulled Ford back to ask him about the day's activities.

I watched as the Duke asked him something. Then Ford asked the Duke something. The Duke pointed at the lieutenant and then at Troll and shrugged his shoulders. Ford paused, put his arms behind his head, wrinkled up his brow, plugged in the facts to his brain, and waited. It was like waiting for a certain program to come up on a computer screen. The light came on quickly for Ford. He spilled out information to the Duke of Earl.

A cloud came over the Duke of Earl's face.

I heard him scream softly. "No."

Obviously what Ford had said was not pleasing to the Duke of Earl. I shuddered. I wanted to run back to the end of the squad to find out what Ford had said. But that was ridiculous. Ford was no prophet. Still, the Duke of Earl was an educated man and he believed in Ford's deductions.

I decided to forget about it as he headed due west like Lt. Brock said. The lieutenant came up to the front after the trail broadened a little.

177

"Lance Corporal. We are supposed to go north for awhile. It says on my plans we should go 45 degrees north when the trail widens." Lt. Brock looked through his horn-rimmed specs like an old professor would check out his notes for a lecture. But an old professor would have plenty of knowledge to draw upon. That was not a luxury Lt. Brock possessed.

"There is a fork in the trail to the north here at the start, so this must be it," said Lt. Brock happily.

He had said, "This must be it." I wondered if "it" was the right way. The Duke of Earl wondered the same thing.

As we headed north, the Duke stormed up to Lt. Brock. "Begging your pardon, sir, but we have never been down this trail. It was always off limits, sir. Are you sure this is the right one?"

Lt. Brock could have exploded. He didn't. I thought it must be because he was not sure.

"Of course I know where we are going, Sergeant," Lt. Brock stammered.

"This is the only fork at the start. Here. You want to see for yourself?"

"No, sir."

I didn't know it then, but I wish the Duke of Earl had looked at the map.

For those of us on our first patrol, we probably felt like the Cub Scout I had been nearly 15 years before. It was O.K. to sit around in our home and weave leather for moccasins, but it was much better to go on an adventure in the hills surrounding our home.

But, for the veterans like the Duke, Donovan, Sloan, Sheridan, Russell and Ford, it was not a romp in the hills. While Troll had a smile plastered on his face as wide as the Mississippi River -at its start at Lake Itasca in Minnesota- and Mouse and Mitschke were nudging each other in the middle of the pack, like Cub Scouts would, I looked back at the vets. No grins. Furrowed brows with darting eyes, first looking straight down at the trail for trip wires and then far into the distance for any other surprises.

We had been out for nearly five hours and it was high noon. I had a fleeting thought this was where Gary Cooper and his mates start blazing away at the enemy. But the enemy was not out in the hot sun. Something else I didn't know then was that the Viet Cong spent their days in the coolness of a hut or even working at whatever job they had, waiting for the night.

The night.

Their time.

As we walked past men on water buffaloes and women picking the rice out of the square sections of underwater "land," we didn't know if they were friendly or not. But except for many of the hustlers around the big cities, the countryside was not full of people. People stayed in small villages, too, but they rarely ventured outside the perimeter, even to visit other relatives. We found out why.

Lt. Brock looked white as a ghost. He told the squad to stop, probably for his sake more than ours. There was no relief from the heat. No palm or banana trees, which were prevalent in Nam, to find shade.

"Close to 120 degrees," said Ford.

"Now is not the time to be practical with numbers, Ford," said the Duke.

I walked over to the Duke and Ford to try to find out what Ford had told the Duke as we had left camp that morning. I wanted to know what the shocked look on Duke's face meant.

Being an aggressive guy, I got right to the point. "Ford, what did you tell the Duke of Earl this morning?"

"You really want to know, Granny?"

"You bet."

"The Duke said you don't believe in prophecy."

"I didn't say that. What I said was that I didn't believe in superstitions or voodoo."

"You think that's what I do-voodoo?"

"Well, yea, don't you?"

"I'm an engineer from the University of Michigan where I studied statistics and probability and learned to not only figure out the likelihood of putting stuff together, but also I schooled myself to determine people's actions in certain situations."

He paused and got to the point, to my original question.

"When Brock told a new guy to take the point, that was the beginning of a disastrous possibility. But when the

180

lieutenant refused to admit we were going a dangerous way when the Duke questioned him, the equation for today became explosive."

While the squad took drinks of Kool-Aid from their canteens and scarfed down ham and lima beans out of green C-ration cans, Lt. Brock sat alone, studying the map. It looked like his glare was going to wear a hole in the piece of parchment. I thought he must be looking for the right path, not admitting to us or even himself we were going the wrong way. Suddenly, he jumped up and said, "O.K. men, I have found a shortcut to our destination."

"I didn't know we had a destination," said the Duke to me. "I thought we were just supposed to case the same area we always did before to see if anything had changed. But he's the lieutenant."

"Why don't you confront him, Duke?" I said pleadingly.

"Listen, Granny, I got busted from sergeant to private once. I got a wife and a bundle of kids at home. They need a big paycheck to keep rolling. You know what I mean? I can't afford to lose this rank again. Brock is the type of guy who would do something irrational and bust me."

"That's my point," I shot back. "You said yourself he's 'irrational.' Don't you think you should kind of guide him a little?"

"Maybe you're right, man. Let me think about it."

As we headed down Lt. Brock's shortcut, the Duke didn't have time to think about it, because Troll suddenly stopped.

The point man, who is like a scout and a guinea pig at the same time, screeched to a halt.

"I just stepped on something," said Troll.

"What is it, Lance Corporal?" said Lt. Brock.

"I'll find out."

Troll handed me his rifle.

"Just a minute, Troll, I want to get a photo of you on patrol, you know for your kid."

Troll gave me that big smile of his, which was normally on his happy face. This was a guy who had plenty of friends. Everyone liked Troll. It didn't matter whether you were black or white or brown or red-and we had Afro-Americans, white Scandinavians, brown Portuguese like Troll and red Indians-Troll was a little Santa Claus with his paunchy stomach and round face.

Then he started to dig where his foot had hit something unusual. "It felt like a plank," he said.

When he had ripped away the debris, there was a wooden cover- to what we didn't know.

"What should I do now?" asked Troll.

"Let's see what's underneath," said Lt. Brock.

The cover came off easily, almost too easily, I thought.

Once the cover was off we hovered around the hole of darkness. The North Vietnamese had built thousands of tunnels to hide their cache of weapons or to even transport themselves underground without being seen. It was cooler traveling underground, too. The VC were smart. It was their turf, their home court. While we were the heavy favorite to win the war, the home court advantage should have been considered. It wasn't and this day like all 10,000 days of the war, we lost.

"I think it's a tunnel," said Troll.

"Go on down and check it out, Marks." Finally he knew his name.

A voice spoke up.

"Wait."

Duke?

No, it was Ford.

"Lt. Brock. I don't think that's a good idea. We don't know what's down there. Why don't you throw a grenade down there first. That was what Lt. Hardie would always do."

That comparison with Lt. Hardie bridled Brock. "I don't care what Lt. Hardie would do. I'm in charge. What if there are weapons down there? We could use them. Maybe there would be plans for some attack on us. We could use them, too. I'd guess..."

A voice spoke up again.

This time it was the Duke.

"Pretty far-fetched thinking, lieutenant."

The Duke of Earl had forgotten about himself. He was thinking about his fellow Marine.

"If you say one more word you're going to be busted down to private again," said Lt. Brock, who obviously had read the Duke of Earl's record.

"Man, I don't care about my rank. This is not the way to do things out here, sir. You can't go guessing at things. You gotta know. With all due respect, sir, you are wrong. And I'm on record with the press here as saying that. Put it all down, Granny."

I wasn't writing, but every word the Duke of Earl said was etched on my brain.

The green Lt. Brock got redder than a chemically-induced tomato. Then he blew up at the Duke of Earl.

"I have had all I could take from you, Marine."

He was right about one thing. The Duke of Earl was a Marine in the best sense of the word. The Duke was trying to look out for his friend. "When we get back to camp, I am going to recommend that you lose one of those stripes if not all for insubordination. Now Lance Corporal, get down there."

Troll had lost his smile.

He looked at me with a lost look. I'll never forget that face with that look. It was the look of a little boy who was about to be thrown into a pool for the first time when he didn't know how to swim yet.

Troll slipped down to the bottom of the tunnel. He found something. It was what the VC had intended him to find. He tripped a wire and the sound of the explosion still rings in my ears occasionally.

While Lt. Brock went into shock, the Duke told me to hold unto him while he lowered himself down into the tunnel.

"Hold on to my legs, Granny. I'll try to grab Troll. Maybe he's not dead."

When the Duke of Earl brought him up, Troll was writhing in pain, and as quick as a wink that Troll would sometimes give you, he lost consciousness.

"Call Sgt. Aaron at camp and tell them to medivac a chopper to...just a minute, Russell. I gotta find out where we are."

The Duke snatched the map from Lt. Brock who had wet his pants at the shock of the explosion and was sitting Indian-style, sobbing, a basket case on his first patrol. I didn't care about Brock. I did care about Troll, who had just experienced his first patrol, and looked like his last.

"Grid 784020. Go at a 45 degree angle from the southeast corner of the grid and they'll see us," said the Duke.

Russell, who was the radio operator, repeated the directions. When the chopper came like an angry bumblebee, the Navy corpsman took one look at Troll and shook his head. He didn't have to say anything. I knew he was not going to make it. Not going to make it to ever hold his baby girl in his arms or to walk her down the aisle someday as a proud papa on her wedding day.

It was the loudest day and the quietest day I had ever spent in my life and probably will ever spend.

There were 27 more operations that year. I wrote about a lot of guys, and the stories paled in comparison to the feelings I poured into the Troll story.

Sad.

Anger.

Doubt.

The first letter of each of those words was the prevailing, pugnacious and powerful emotion that saddled me the rest of the tour. I will never shake that moment...of losing someone I cared for.

Troll was my friend. Others died, not your friends.

Back in Minnesota I had been spared as a teen-ager from the experience of losing a friend in a car accident or to a disease like leukemia. In my family only my mom's mother, Gaga, had died. I remember her funeral as a sad time where my mom and her two sisters, Isabelle and Sylvia, cried over the casket of their mother.

I never was able to cry at the casket of Troll. I never even saw his dead body. It was whisked away too fast in the chopper, a symbol of death as far as I was concerned.

I never even saw the death notice, which I thought was strange, but then facts don't add up in the rice paddies and tunnels of Vietnam. I never received the final word on Troll until 27 years later when I went to the Vietnam War Memorial-the Wall where all the names of the war dead are listed-but that's another story.

CHAPTER 20

Prejudice leads to death

One of the saddest parts of the Marines is that there was plenty of prejudice-even in a war zone.

The blacks and whites were still separated in the Land of the Yellow Hordes just like they were in the Land of the Statue of Liberty.

Despite this prejudice around us, Sgt. Aaron, who I said I had dubbed "Ponds"(after the brand name of a skin cream) because of his "smooth" wisdom, and I became fast friends. Aaron had a special affinity for Mouse, like we all did.Being the smallest guy, he was always being picked on.

In the middle of June we were all drinking at the NCO club that had been set up at our base camp. A sergeant decided that Mouse had enough to drink and cut him off.

Aaron got in a brawl with this guy for cutting his buddy off. Aaron was fortunate nothing ever came of the fight. He could have demolished a fine record, but Aaron didn't seem to care about his personal record, but he did care about his friends. For a moment, though, I doubted his wisdom and wondered about his anger.

I had never seen an explosion from Aaron before. He had always kept his cool. I was the one who felt ready to sizzle at a drop of an insult.

Not Aaron.

Most guys you could figure. You could count on what they would do or not do.

Three guys come to mind, all of whom I wrote about in individual profiles which my commanding officer liked and kept asking for more. It made me closer to some guys-and it hurt more when they were killed. Like Casey.

You know the poem by Thayer called "Casey at the Bat."

In the poem Casey struck out.

In Vietnam, Casey struck out, too.

The unit I was with-1st battalion, 11th Marines-had been asked to support the infantry unit of B battery, 3rd battalion, 1st Marines. It was February, three days after Valentine's Day and only three weeks after losing Troll. Why did people say bad things come in threes? In my case, it was true.

Lt. Blair, who was forward observer that day, sent the word to fire six rounds into a likely enemy mortar position.

Lt. Blair had called in coordinates 996444 and the first one and the third through the sixth ones all hit that target. But not the second one. It hit at 996217 or about 200 meters short of the enemy position.

Short round.

Short round to Marines are two dangerous words because it normally means that something was miscalculated and the round will fall "short" of its intended target- the enemy position- and will hit your defensive position.

PFC Donald Green, who was green when it came to experience in life like most 19-year-old average kids- never knew what hit him.

I know. I was next to him.

The crater caused by the short artillery round was examined by Lt. Blair the next day. The dimensions were six feet in diameter and three feet deep.

I received a concussion from the blast, but Green received a free trip home in a pine box. Green and Casey were friends. They had known each other all their lives, growing up together, playing baseball and then joining the Marines.

Casey was always the hero, looking out for Green, who not only did not have the physical prowess Casey possessed, but also did not have the smarts. Casey could have lorded it over his friend, but instead he became "big brother."

So, that night we went out on patrol to the same area we had been the night before. When Casey, who had just come back from R&R in Hong Kong, found out from Lt. Blair what had happened he went berserk.

"Why did you send in the rounds anyway?" screamed Casey at the lieutenant.

I was standing between the two, watching another explosion. But I wasn't ready for what happened next.

Ashen, Lt. Blair stammered, I..I...I thought the spot was a likely enemy position I thought..."

"You thought, man; you can't think; you gotta know. You have to make sure. Where is the enemy? Can you see him?"

Trying to calm Casey suddenly became Lt. Blair's target. Casey was his enemy. He was standing in the way of his rank. It was a mistake in judging human character. Lt. Blair didn't get to know his men. He just expected them to obey him.

"Casey, you must calm down. I want you to report back to the base camp."

It was 2000 or 8 at night and that in itself was a stupid suggestion. No one goes around Gookland at night-by himself. No one was going to tell Casey what to do that night either.

"I'm not going anywhere until I find the enemy. I want my friend to know he didn't die for nothing."

Like Casey at the bat, the Marine Casey snatched his lumber- an M-14 rifle, which was being used before we received our toy plastic M-16 rifles.

"Where was the enemy, lieutenant?"

The lieutenant faltered a bit. He fumbled through his pockets. "Here is the call. Check it yourself."

He threw the paper at Casey. Casey read hastily and started off. Trying to regain control was the worst thing Lt. Blair did at that moment. Because he tried to regain control so he won, not so everyone won. Blair was selfish. It cost him.

"Casey, you're not going anywhere. I order you to come back here."

Then he added, "Stop or I'll shoot."

Casey kept walking toward where he thought the enemy was. Then Lt. Blair made a fatal mistake. He fired a round through Casey's arm. Like the athlete he was, Casey whirled and faced his new enemy, and blew away the lieutenant.

With one arm dangling at his side, he carried his bat over his uninjured shoulder. With blood gushing from the wound, he completed the 200-meter dash, not in record time, but he found the "likely enemy position," where there was no sign of the enemy. So, he went further into the jungle, seeking to destroy the enemy.

I had watched all this in horror half-dazed. Despite the concussion 24 hours before, I had gone out again. Green had died the night before. Now Blair was dead. And Casey would be too, if I didn't radio my friend Aaron, who was back at the base camp. I didn't know if he had been the fire direction officer who had figured out the elevations and deflections the night before. I hoped he hadn't. If so, he had been part of a muddled mess of murder, which had almost cost his best friend's life.

"Aaron," I screamed into the radio, which I had snatched like it was the greatest belated Valentine's Day gift I could receive.

"Granny? Is that you? What's wrong?"

"After last night when my brains oozed out I thought I would never be thinking again. But now I have to."

"What are you talking about, man?"

I figured Aaron must have heard what had happened the night before because an investigation had begun that morning by Lt. Blair.

"Blair has been shot. Casey did it."

"Is this one of your tall tales? You're kidding, right?"

"This time I'm serious, Aaron. Help me."

I pleaded with Aaron to send someone after Casey. The rest of the platoon had gone to another position and only Lt. Blair knew where they were. And Lt. Blair wasn't talking. Ever.

"Casey headed for that position where the artillery hit last night. Tell someone to follow him, but be careful. He's over the edge. He could kill anybody who stood in his way."

"I'll tell the C.O., Granny. Are you O.K.?"

"Oh, I'll be all right," I lied.

I got help, although Aaron said I was always slightly crazier after that night. Aaron waited awhile to go crazy. He was stronger than I was.

Casey?

No one ever found him. It was probably just as well. He would have faced a court martial and been placed in prison for killing an officer. Yet, I still think he was insane at the time. When I think of Casey, I remember a guy who loved his friend. My next thought was vicious. If that's striking out, maybe everyone should strike out for a friend. Was I condoning Casey's actions? Was I like Casey? Had I struck out in my Marine mind?

CHAPTER 21

Traded to Red Sox and then traded again-back to Yankees

In 1971 my minor league career had not struck out. Rather it was on the upswing. But like I said, my career did continue its roller coaster ride.

I was traded. To the Red Sox.

When that happens, it's like you just received a blow in the head, which I knew all about. Maybe it was because Billy G. was no longer around to sing my praises. But I also knew that the big league manager of the Yankees, Mark Proctor, did not like Billy. I believe he was scared Billy would take his place. Now that Billy was no longer a threat alive, he thought his favorite player might be. So, I heard through the grapevine that my days were numbered. I started the 1972 season with a down attitude. But that quickly changed when Ted Williams, not only the greatest Red Sox hitter ever but also probably the all-time best student of hitting, came into camp and talked about hitting a baseball. He said to use a slightly up swing when you hit the ball. Since it was spring when all things spring eternal, I thought I'd try a different style. With my speed, other coaches had told me to hit ground balls and beat 'em out. Sometimes I listened and sometimes I didn't.

My new surroundings did not stop my rise from A ball at Lynchburg at the beginning of the year to AA ball at New Britain at the end of the year. My average skyrocketed to .497 in 30 days at New Britain. By the next year I was in my seventh year in the minors and 30 years old. And, still not in the majors. I told Alex that if I didn't make it to the bigs by the following year I was going to try something else.

"What would you do?" asked her father, A.A., at Christmas time when we went there for the holidays.

"I can write. I did some stuff for the college newspaper. When I was there I had an ancient teacher, Enoch Keenan, who always encouraged me. He would tell me to be clear about my writing. Say what "it" and "they" meant. But he would say he liked my 'stuff,' as he called it, I mean my stories." Since I had been in baseball I had time to play golf in the mornings before night games. I had become pretty good at that sport, too.

Always the battler I was.

I knew I could compete.

Once one of my golfing buddies, Jimmy Kerwin, put a buck down behind the hole and said he would bet me that dollar I couldn't make a putt from the fringe of the green. I concentrated so hard on that putt that you could have taken a picture of me while I was putting and I would not have heard the click of the camera. The ball went in the jar. I figured if I could concentrate like that I could try the golf tour.

"Maybe I'll go from one pro sport to another, Mr. P."

"What's that?"

"Golf."

"Are you that good?"

"I guess I will have to wait and see. Most guys don't try the pro golf tour after they are 30. Most of them are just out of college. But being the Lone Ranger has never stopped me before. I don't care if anyone else is doing it. I figure what's best for me and assess my abilities and hopefully my decision is right."

However, that year my concentration was on baseball, not golf.

I was sure I would be picked to play with the Red Sox and visit Fenway Park and its Green Monster left field wall with the Citgo sign over the screen.

I would be hitting the wall with my best stroke soon. With that kind of vision I hit .370 in 1973.

That was in Triple A at Pawtucket.

I headed up the roller coaster to what I thought was the peak.

The ultimate.

The majors. The promised land.

I was sure I would be called up because there was no one on the major league roster who could play center field like I could.

Then the roller coaster not only took a twist downward but also sent me off the track in what I had chosen as my profession-baseball.

I was traded.

Back to the Yankees.

Where the major league manager Mark Proctor didn't want anything to do with me.

No one in the Red Sox organization made it clear to me when they traded me. They just said it's part of baseball. But I found out the reason in the Boston Globe the morning after I was traded. A story by one of the beat reporters who covered the Red Sox daily had talked to the minor league coordinator because he thought it was a strange move to trade such an all around kid.

However, what the sports writer found out was that the Red Sox had somebody better, they thought. In the classification below me there was a center fielder by the name of Fred Lynn, who the minor league scouts said was destined for greatness. And he was 21. I was 10 years older. A year later the scouts were proved right as Lynn took over most of the headlines by playing a flawless center field, hitting .331 with 21 homers and 105 runs batted in. He became the first player ever to be given both the rookie-of-the-year and the MVP award in his first season. Boston won the American League pennant and forgot all about old man Moses. Old at 32?

In baseball some think so, but I wasn't ready to quit. I remembered my pop's "Never Give Up" words clearly.

The Moses trip to the Promised Land was temporarily set back I thought. Where we went next was more like the Land of Football and Golf, though. Alex and I and our two kids, Joy and Arnold, found the newest place to live in Columbus, Ohio, full of sports fans, but they followed the exploits of the Ohio State Buckeyes and their great football coach Woody Hayes and when the gridiron was not being watched with the keen eye during the summer it was Jack Nicklaus and how their hometown boy had become the dominant player in golf.

And baseball didn't even finish third. Theme parks had become instantaneous hits and families headed for the one in Columbus rather than watch the baseball team play.

After all, we were minor league. Woody and Jack weren't. While it may be tough to play in front of scant home crowds and still try to keep your enthusiasm up, the minors are places where you have to rev up your motor daily. You can decide how that day is going to go. At least you can decide to be positive. I knew I would strike out. I had done that many times after that day against Custer when I was 10 years old. But my pop had lifted me up out of the water and out of despair. I would not drown in self pity again, I thought at the time. Still, Vietnam memories hammered at me.

Columbus was great for our family in 1974. Well, maybe I thought it was great because I hammered the ball at a .359 clip and again I thought I would reach the Promised Land.

Mickey Mantle had retired in 1969 and a kid named Bobby Murcer was supposed to be the next Mick. He became a $100,000 player. But he never became another Mickey. But in the winter of 1974 he was traded for another $100,000 player, Bobby Bonds. Bonds eventually became one of those 30-30 guys, who like Willie Mays combined speed-30 stolen bases- with power-30 home runs. I was destined to spend another year in Columbus.

A few years before I had read about an Olympic sprinter, Bobby Morrow, who felt he had reached his peak at age 32. The article had said a man reached his physical peak from age 28-32. I was 32. I knew if I hadn't reached my peak at that time, I never would.

I pressed extra hard in spring training of 1975. I swung and missed a lot in spring training and I was switched to right field, which was unfamiliar to me, where I dropped a fly ball after hitting the wall and laid unconscious for several minutes as New York Yankee Manager Mark Proctor watched.

I was disheartened after the game when I heard him tell one of the Yankee coaches, Larry Berra, he didn't know what Billy Golenbeck saw in me. Larry, though, had been a close friend of Billy's. He could tell I was pressing. He knew I could hit, run and fly after the ball.

"Moses can play. He's just playing too hard."

You had to speak "Yogi," which was Berra's nickname, to understand him, but he meant I was trying too hard.

"Send him out to Columbus again after tomorrow's game with the Cardinals in St. Petersburg's Al Lang Field," growled Proctor as he chomped his favorite meal, a submarine sandwich.

Since Berra had been so close to Billy Golenbock before he was killed in a car accident, and he knew how much Billy liked me, he thought he would do me a favor. He told me what Proctor was going to do the next day. But he didn't just hand me the bitter news on a rusty platter and let me digest it by myself.

He gave me some Yogi advice.

"Listen, Moses. I know Billy thought you had the heart to play in the big leagues. And I always agreed with Billy, even when I didn't."

Translated from Yogi, he meant he might have disagreed at first with Billy, but because of Billy's superior knowledge of people and the game of baseball, he would change his mind and go on Billy's side.

"If you go all out, even hustle all the time, tomorrow maybe Proctor will change his mind. What do you think?"

"O.K., Yogi, I'll give it my best shot."

I laughed at his double positive-all out and hustle all the time.

HITTING THE WALL

"Yea, I'll do what you say."

Yogi made sure I was in the lineup the next day.

He had inserted me in the batting order at leadoff, my best spot.

CHAPTER 22

Soul brothers; introduction to a little girl named Hope

As I knocked the dirt off my spikes with my Jackie Robinson bottle bat made by Louisville Slugger, I thought about my friend Aaron. Robinson had broken the color line in 1947 when he became the first black man to play major league baseball. Aaron had not broken any color lines, but he had been a leader in Vietnam. Lt. Hardie always asked his advice about the different black guys in the battalion. Lt. Hardie considered "Ponds" a smooth operator when it came to fixing any problem the lieutenant might have with a soul brother. And "Ponds" usually could find a way that wasn't harsh to "smooth" out the problem.

Usually.

One time he wasn't able to grease the skids for his brothers. That was when Russell Cosby blew away a white guy who called him a "nigger." Lt. Hardie talked with Aaron about it. I saw Aaron go into the tent to talk with the lieutenant and I waited outside in the hot sand for about 30 minutes. Usually their discussions were short, Aaron said.

"He listens, really listens to what I have to say. I wish my father would listen like Lt. Hardie."

"My father doesn't really listen to me either, Ponds, because he's too busy giving advice. But that's the way fathers are."

"Maybe, but I still wish..."

I had the bad habit of interrupting people, but then I also couldn't hear very well. After that shell exploded in Vietnam, I lost about 30 percent of my hearing. But I didn't find that out until long after the stint in southeast Asia.

"So, what happened in there?"

"You know about Russell?"

"Yea, I'd heard. He shot a guy because he called him a 'nigger.'"

"Lt. Hardie said he couldn't really help Russell. That murder couldn't be negotiated. That he couldn't listen to the fact that he knew the white guy shouldn't have been prejudiced. That Russell would serve a sentence in prison and then be dishonorably discharged."

Before I could say interrupt, Aaron exploded in anger.

"Why in hell do white dudes hate us for our color? Why in God's name is that, Moses?"

Tears started coming down his cheeks.

I couldn't answer my friend Aaron. I didn't have an answer.

He turned on his heels of his camouflage rice patty stompers.

He wheeled off.

"Where you going, Aaron?"

"To get bombed, Moses."

He didn't ask me to come along like he usually did.

"I'm coming with you."

"No, man, stay away."

"Sorry, man, I can't hear you."

I laughed and that broke the flow of anger. Aaron reached down and put his arm around me. "O.K., little buddy, I'm going to need you to carry me back to my tent."

The thought of a 5-6 guy carrying a 6-6 guy across the sands of Vietnam was too much for me. I started laughing so hard I shook and fell down in the sand holding my sides.

I got into the batter's box, ready now for the pitch. Though I was near my dream, I had not reached it yet.

My friend Aaron had struggled just as much as I had since Vietnam, not living in the same city for long and not holding a job for long. Aaron had not been climbing. He had been falling. My friend Aaron had not catapulted his career as a leader as a sergeant in the Marines to a force back in the States. His oldest brother had risen to the top or was trying to as a mayor of a major metropolis. His second brother was forging his way as a member of this strong family by helping his brother as a spokesman similar to Bobby helping John Kennedy when the older brother ran for President in 1960. When you have those types of strong family members to follow you would think that the third son would be a stable link as well. Although Aaron had been on a roller coaster like I had, his highs and lows had been steeper. He and his wife Maddy had two kids but they were as different as their two parents. While Aaron showed both leadership and emotion he could not seem to separate the two. He had a hard time with both characteristics because he did not feel he was a leader because he was the third son and a junior. He had grown up with a critical mind, which is good at solving problems in Vietnam, but not good when it comes to giving honor to your wife and not bringing your children to anger. Aaron had gone back to an old neighborhood in Augusta where drug dealing was one way to make a living and had become involved with old friends, although his mother said they were not his friends.

"You're the only friend Junior has ever had," she said after we got back from Nam.

Maddy, on the other hand, walked the straight line in life. Aaron had struggled with jobs, graduating second from a job service school, and then refusing to take a menial position. Although Aaron did not think too much of himself, he had been taught by his folks to reach for the sky. Running a continental can line was not his idea of the stars. In act, it was reaching to the bottom of the barrel to pick out strips of metal that were turned into cans of beans. Aaron did not want to be chomping on beans and franks the rest of his life. He wanted steak and baked potatoes. So he joined a small gang. Gangs like guys who are 6-6. But Maddy allowed him to try to find his way after going through a war, not pushing him, wishing and hoping like the song from Dusty Springfield said. But she became tired of waiting after a half dozen years and had left him, following the track her husband could have taken-in politics. She saw what Aaron's older brother was climbing-the golden ladder she thought- and she jumped on, chasing the American dream that Martin Luther King, Jr. had talked about. So, after Aaron had quit the job at the continental can company and then left another job as a TV technician, where the people thought he could fix anything, he went into a different type of "fix business," and Maddy, fearing for her two little girls lives, fled her husband.

I didn't really blame her.

One of the gang members didn't sell drugs. He was the enforcer.

And Maddy did not want anyone enforcing on her and her two girls.

The oldest girl, Hope, had leadership ability with a body full of emotion. She was like her daddy. She could tell you what to do with such fervor you thought she was the adult and you were the child. This Hope was an ostentatious orator.

One time Hope and I were talking about her daddy and I asked her if she wanted to be like him when she grew up.

Hope went into such a tirade that I thought I was talking with an octopus as she flung her arms in constant gestures to make her point.

"Listen, Mr. Godfather."

She would always start her sentences with "listen," because she loved to imitate Charles Stanley, a Baptist minister from Atlanta, who always would tell his audience to "listen" to grab their attention. Both in Stanley's and Hope's case, the quirk worked. She called me "Godfather" because Aaron had asked me to watch out for his little girl if anything ever happened to him. When you go through a war, you think something bad is going to happen to you.

Suddenly.

Soon.

Anyway, Hope said, "No, I hope to be a R&B (Rhythm and Blues) star like Aretha Franklin. I got this powerful voice that can boom all the way to the back row in church so I figure I can reach the back row of big stadiums when I perform on stage when I'm old enough."

Before I could ask her how old was "old enough," she continued her pulsations.

"Listen, if you had the power I got than you would use it, wouldn't you?" Again she didn't wait for a reply. "Do you use your power-down deep here?" She pointed to her heart. "Listen, Mr. Godfather, you have not been hitting too many homers lately. That's what the newspaper, the Atlanta

207

Constitution, said when they were talking about prospects for the majors."

I marveled at Hope. Six years old and talking like a grown-up. Forget that she knew the word "prospect." She knew that you were supposed to give your "heart" and soul to life. Her sister Idona was industrious and a constant worker like her mother. But it was Hope who carried the emotional banner from her father. When you're emotional, that characteristic can send you reeling if you hit a brick wall.

I wondered if Aaron had hit his brick wall, selling drugs. I knew he was trying to forget the war. Maybe he wanted to forget that night when a Marine was killed by a short round and I was nearly blown away. I would have to ask him if he was on duty that night.

CHAPTER 23

Hope had told her godfather he could cash in on the diamond-does he?; another close friend and teammate shares his story of faith and guides him in another direction

Now, though, I needed to get on base and show some of that heart that Hope had dangled in my memory.

I checked the defense. Against a right handed pitcher I was batting left handed so the opposing team had switched around to the right for me like so many foes had in the past. I liked when they pulled around to one side because then I could spank the ball through the holes the shift had created.

Glory days.

Sun shining in Florida. I felt like a red tomato already, but I felt good. I was going to change the mind of Mark Proctor and make him keep me. I was going to show him.

A slight wind moved the leaves of the palm trees as a sparse northern crowd who had trekked down south settled into their seats. The wind sent a chill through me. Funny, I thought, I shouldn't be shivering in Florida.

The first pitch came in whistling. The ball blasted into the catcher's well-oiled leather glove. Boy, did that smell good. I figured the second pitch would be another fast ball. The pitcher didn't want to be fancy early on. The next pitch was a duplicate of the first except this time I was like Hope's octopus act as I swung my arms into action. Since I was little rusty I swung late, but I swung hard and sent the ball on a line over the third baseman's head. The left fielder was way over toward center, so I was headed for second from home plate. As I raced toward second I watched the ball like Willie Mays did when he ran the bases. The left fielder knocked the ball down, but had trouble picking up the 5 oz. sphere, so I shifted into a higher gear.

Boom!

The short round hit again. I was in pain again. This time a chopper didn't take me away. An ambulance did.

"Sorry, Jock," said the team physician, Dr. Lee Latimer, in the emergency room of the hospital in St. Petersburg, "but you blew a hamstring. You'll be out for a week. Make sure and rest. We'll ice it for a couple days to keep the swelling down. Then rest, remember!"

I couldn't believe it. The next week was a long seven days. In fact, I came back a day early. I have always been short on patience.

When I arrived at the field that day I was in for a big surprise. One of the friendliest guys I had ever known had joined the camp. His name was Chico Durand. He was a veteran ballplayer, too. Back in 1965 we had known each other at Greensboro before I headed for the Marines and he went into the air force. While I had gone overseas, he had stayed in Omaha, Nebraska as a weather observer. Chico was a great observer of mankind, too. He saw the intensity I had and since he had the same characteristic we became friends. Chico was half Puerto Rican and half English. He spoke in half Latin American and half British, a truly unique style. Chico had a unique style on the diamond, too. He had played shortstop when I first saw him, but he had "hands of stone," and the coaches shifted him to the outfield.

He had a rocket arm, throwing the ball over the fence and into the cornfields that surrounded the park. The arm- and his ability to play infield or outfield and even catcher once in awhile- kept him around the minors and eventually he had a cup of coffee in the majors with the Minnesota Twins, who liked to sign Latin American players for a cup of coffee and a dozen Dunkin' Donuts. The owner was a cheapskate.

Chico saw me first.

"Heh, man, I know you. You were that fast guy back in North Carolina. You were...heh, what's the matter, why are you limping?"

I looked at this sensitive stump of a guy. I was good at names. I smiled. "Chico. Why are you here? Are you still playing? It's been 10 years. I saw your name in the box scores with the Twins a few times. What was it like?"

I had completely ignored his question about the hamstring pull. I didn't want to think about it.

"Yea, man, I'm still horsing around. Yea, it was great to travel first class. Coming from where I do-you remember travel by horseback not jet planes and paper shacks not fancy hotels. The Twins were finally starting to pay better and then I get traded to the Yankees."

Then he added, "Well, it's great to see a familiar face. Moses, right?"

"Right. Jock Moses. Chico Durand, right?"

"You have a good memory. How about your game? Is speed still your cup of tea?"

"Still is, Chico, but..."

"What? Is it your leg?"

"Exactly. I pulled a hamstring but I'm still hoping to get another chance. I've never played an inning in the bigs."

"I heard they're going to post the final cut today, Moses."

I went into shock. I wasn't aware of that.

Without saying a word, I raced to the list of major and minor league assignments that was posted on two huge bulletin boards. After checking for my name on the major league roster and not finding it, I was afraid that I would find "Jock Moses" on the minor league list. My fears were affirmed.

As I stared at my name, I felt a hand on my shoulder. "Great, man, we're both going to be assigned to Columbus."

I shook off his hand and faced him, filled with anger.

"I come back a day early. I give my all and they reward me with a demotion. I'm never going to make it."

"You have to accept what happens in life, Moses. You can only give your best. I still have visions of a little blur going around the bases in North Carolina. Now you can rip through Ohio. Never give up, man."

He made me smile like my Pop used to do. And he echoed my father's words to "never give up." He had not retreated when I blasted him. He stayed with me in that discouraging moment. A friend was there when you needed him, I thought.

Chico Durand turned out to be a friend forever.

Even though I didn't rip through Ohio.

The time in Columbus with Chico was one of relaxation. I hadn't relaxed ever since I started my quest for the top. Chico and I would play golf in the mornings before our night games. While he was almost as skinny as a thermometer, Chico could pound the ball 300 yards, although not always in the right direction. When it came to our friendship he was right down the middle and always on target.

While my game on the diamond deteriorated because my hamstring was not healing and my batting average slumped to .216, the lowest of my career, I really never hit bottom emotionally. And Chico Durand was the reason. I missed my friend Aaron, who had skidded into drugs. Maddy had divorced him when he slugged her for talking to another man. This man who was a leader in the toughest of situations had fallen apart. I had not been able to pick up the pieces of our relationship, which made me sad. But Chico filled that void.

One morning when we were on the golf course before the greens had dried out and before the wind started to blow, Chico whetted my appetite with a spirited idea that blew my mind.

We had played 13 holes and I led Chico by six shots with five holes to play. He couldn't beat me.

"I hit the ball 300 yards and you kill me," laughed Chico, running his hand through prematurely gray hair. "You keep missing the green. You live on the fringe, man." We had to laugh at that joke because his comment had a double meaning. I would always hit short of the green and land on the fringe. Then I would chip close enough for one putt and sometimes knock the ball in the cup with my trusty sand wedge. But living on the fringe not only meant making a living on the fringe of the green, but it could mean making a living on the edge.

I had been living on the edge of my goal of being a big league ballplayer, but hadn't made it.

Chico saw my ability in another area-golf.

Taking golf seriously was not in my thought pattern because it was fun. But Chico measured my possible greatness in other arenas beside Fenway Park or Yankee Stadium. He saw me at St. Andrews or Augusta National.

After the round that day, Chico reiterated his thoughts about my switching careers to the links.

"You have the competitive spirit to make it, I believe, Jock. Golfers bloom later than baseball players. Speaking of spirit, do you have The Spirit?"

"What do you mean, Chico? The Spirit of God?"

"Yeh."

"I once had a buddy ask me about finding peace with God. I'm not sure I have found that. Now you ask me about the Spirit of God. It's confusing trying to figure out how to get peace or who God is or what is the Spirit."

"For some guys they battle with their relationship with God all their lives. For others, it is a simple acceptance. You're like a bantam rooster, Jock. You want to fight, eh?"

"I never really thought I was fighting God, but maybe I want to see some good things happen to me before I follow Him."

"You're married, aren't you?"

"Yea. With two kids."

"Those aren't good things?"

I thought back to when I was given extra courage to not have sex with Janie. That was a good thing. My Pop used to tell me in all other religions you went to God. In Christianity, God came to you. I realized the extra courage came from a God who knew my future and wanted me to marry Alex. Today. Right now. I had the best.

Chico seemed to know what I was thinking.

"With what you got right now, Moses. You got to accept what you got right now. Then you'll find peace and your love for your Creator will soar and maybe that Spirit will expand your love toward yourself and others. You seem down a lot of times, yet you don't give up. I admire the last part, but wonder why you still hang on to the negative thoughts. You're beating yourself up."

"I know I am beating myself up in the quest to be a major leaguer. You really think I could make a golf pro?"

"I know the ability is there, but I don't know if God wants you there."

"O. K. I'll check into the qualifying school."

"Remember, Jock, I can't look into the future. Maybe you won't make it. But if you don't, I know you'll make some friends along the way. And you have that don't quit attitude, which will lead you in another direction. Whatever you do, trust God to direct your paths."

CHAPTER 24

Leaving the hope of a diamond career

My folks had always told me about God. They walked their talk. Alexandra rarely voiced her faith, but she sure lived close to God's heart, I thought. I wanted to use the abilities God had given me, but since I was a perfectionist I thought I should always reach the top in whatever I did. Doing my best wasn't good enough. I had to be the best in games, relationships, whatever came in my path. That was not a peaceful way to live. The spirit I had within me was not a calm breeze but an irascible tornado that not only sent my life spinning like Dorothy's farm house in "The Wizard of Oz," but also shook the foundations of people around me.

Since my hamstring injury had put me on the disabled list, I didn't have to come to the park each night. I went that night to tell the manager I was going to leave baseball. It was hard to leave the park, but even more difficult was leaving the guys, like Chico.

"You'll be the best Jock Moses if you follow His path," Chico reminded me. "Keep in touch, man."

I told Chico that the qualifying school was still 3 months away, but that would give my hamstring time to heal and me enough time to prepare. I could still use a cart and hit golf balls.

There were two cuts you had to make to receive a PGA tour card. The first was a district qualifying at different sites around the country. If you made the top 25, you then came to Florida for the national qualifying. The top 25 from that school would then be eligible the next year. It was the middle of July and I had found the closest school was Quincy, Illinois, a town on the Mississippi River, just up from Mark Twain's famous hometown of Hannibal, Missouri.

The district qualifying was four rounds. With two holes left, I needed a birdie and a par to make it. The 17th hole was a par three and as I normally did I hit the ball short on the fringe. It was slightly uphill, so instead of my trusty sand wedge I chose an 8-iron so the ball would run a little farther. The ball took off like a rocket and banged off the stick and into the hole.

Birdie.

The final hole was a dogleg right par four. Since I fade the ball slightly it was a perfect setup for me. I spanked that baby right to the right corner, shortening my second shot to the green. However, true to form, I hit the ball on the fringe again, making it tougher for me to par the hole. But the sand wedge clipped the ball within 12 inches of the hole.

Par.

Now I had just over four months to get ready for the national tourney in Florida early in December. I used that time by practicing so hard my hands bled. Then I would tape them up and go out and hit some more balls. Some people called that hitting the wall while running a marathon. You know, you hit the wall of discouragement and you can't seem to go any farther, but you find your second wind and go on. You NEVER GIVE UP!

Even though I was alone often that year, concentrating by myself on the practice range, it gave me time to think about what really counted most to me- my family.

Another addition to our family that year had put extra pressure on me to support them.

His name was Ben, a Vietnamese orphan. Alex and I had seen a documentary the previous summer and we had decided to adopt a Vietnamese child. When Saigon fell on April 30, 1975, we received notification three days later that there was a little boy for us. We could pick him up at the airport the following day.

All Ben had on when he came to us was a pair of white shorts and a brown-and-white striped shirt. He had tossed his sneakers out the window of the car on the way to the airport in Denver where he had flown from. The next morning when I tried to take off his clothes to get him dressed for church at Forest Lutheran, a tiny old-fashioned congregation of about 40 members, he screamed because he thought I was stealing all he had.

Thankfully Ben and I got to trust each other a little more after that.

So, I went into the national tournament with a little more to shoot for now that I had three kids to support.

There were six rounds this time.

In the first round I was paired with Roger and Dave Fleming, who were twins from Burlington, Wisconsin, an unlikely place for golfers. I thought the major sport in Wisconsin was deer hunting. You'd be better off choosing to be a butcher of deer meat than trying to make it as a golfer. Of course, I forgot that I came from farther north than the Flemings. But why ruin the story with the facts?

With us in the foursome was Bob Amen. I loved that name. When I met this tall, gaunt gentleman, whose white hair and gimpy stride made him look like he was gaining on 50 years of age, I had to tease him about his last name.

"I bet you get a lot of prayers said for you. Amen brother!"

I cracked up. The Flemings shook their heads collectively.

Bob waited until the laughter subsided and then got me back with, "That kind of thinking comes up rather short, just like you."

Since I had just scraped by in the district qualifying school, I should have figured I was a long shot for the nationals. Somehow I missed that mathematical formula. I wasn't even close to securing my PGA tour card. I missed the top 25 by 18 strokes. I didn't have a stroke, though, because I remembered what Chico had told me about accepting what happens and that I would make friends. The latter part turned out to be true because the Flemings and Amen are still friends. But that's another story.

I went back to Columbus where Alex had been staying in an apartment, which is normal for minor leaguers and their families. Even though we had rented a house once, we did not dare buy a house because we were always pulling up stakes and moving from town to town. We almost lived out of a suitcase. I asked Alex where she wanted to go.

"I'll go wherever you need to go, Jock," she said in her normal acceptance of our tumultuous travels since we had been married.

"I guess it will have to be where I can find a job. The sports editor in Quincy, Illinois, where I made district qualifying, mentioned to me that if I didn't make it on the PGA tour that he needed someone to cover golf, which would be right down my fairway, and high school sports, which I would love doing. I mean, I love kids."

221

I looked at Joy, Arnold and Ben. Ben had been with us since May and was about to celebrate his first Christmas- with snow- with us. He loved the first snowfall. He went outside and ran around with his tongue out to try to catch the snowflakes as they sifted down from the heavens.

I looked at Ben with a sense of sorrow because he had been tossed around a war zone before coming to America. Now it appeared he would continue in another battle. The social worker had called right before Christmas. She had said Ben's mother was in country and wanted him back.

The next year would be involved in court battles. What happened to Ben is another story.

CHAPTER 25

Moving to Quincy, Illinois and writing up a storm; moving again to Minnesota to become a teacher; a second daughter is born

Stories became my life for a year and a half because the sports editor in Quincy still needed another staff member. We moved to Quincy where we found a nice little white brick house with roses growing along a strip between the house and the driveway. Joy loved watering them; well, you know that story-sometimes she was as soaked as they were.

I jumped right into the golf scene, creating a column called "Hats Off to Golf," and encouraging kids in all sports, although Quincy High School basketball was the top game in town. That was due to the all-encompassing coach Sherrill Hanks, who had won 20 games for 13 consecutive years, and once finished second in the Illinois state tourney to eventual Olympian and pro defensive genius Quinn Buckner's high school team.

I asked him what it was like to feel the pressure of having to win 20 every season. "Coming through under pressure," he mused, "is what life is all about. Don't you think so, Jock?"

I thought over that question, remembering I just had failed at making the majors in baseball and qualifying for the pro golf tour, and wondered if I had missed what life was all about. I had not come through under pressure, including my relationship with my best friend Aaron, or the guy who used to be my best friend. I had not been there for him like Chico Durand had helped me in a tough time or even the golfing friends I had found in Florida.

I figured the deadline pressures I felt in my new position would be immeasurably less than a short artillery round, which had killed one man and almost knocked me off, and should be even easier than trying to smack a fastball from Bob Gibson, the Cardinals right hander who I had faced in spring training in St. Petersburg, Florida when I was with the Yankees.

I was right. I thrived on this pressure. But I wasn't making a whole lot of money. Our check book was down to $100. The minor leagues had paid around $6,000 a year, so all through those years Alex had to work as a nurse to keep our heads above water. Her strength was money management. She cut out coupons, sent in rebates and saved us about $3,000 a year. Then Alex got pregnant. I loved the job. Managing editor Charlie Barnum said I could stay as long as he was there, but he understood I had to take care of my family. He had been a journalism professor at Northwestern and said college life is a great place for raising a family.

"Jock, let me check to see if there are apprenticeships around. You like writing about kids. Ever thought about teaching?"

"Yes, Mr. Barnum, I did consider teaching and coaching when I was back at the University of Minnesota, but I had not taken any education courses by the time graduation rolled around. Then I got the surprise of my life when I was signed by the Yankees and all those ideas were tossed in the back of my mind."

Mr. Barnum's comment about a college atmosphere being a nice place to raise a family sank into my thought process like a scoop of ice cream in a Root Beer Float. The result was that I told Alex to pack her bags again. We were going back to the University of Minnesota.

That was not an easy task since she was eight months pregnant, which was why I was thinking about my family and not my job. Alex never buckled under the strain of shifting homes. She cried with her friends in Quincy- Dick and Mae Shierling across the street helped us pack boxes and my mother came down from Minnesota to help us move closer to her home. Now in the Twin Cities we would be less than 100 miles away from my mother and father where we had been about 500 in Quincy.

Alex did her part too. Being a night owl, she stayed up to 3 in the morning the night before we were supposed to move to give our dog Ellie Mae a bath. Ellie Mae, a wire-haired fox terrier, was named after the TV character, Ellie Mae Clampett of the Beverly Hillbillies. She had been given to us by a couple from Florida who had moved to Quincy. We had become friends just because we had spent time in Florida in my minor league days.

My mother had to laugh at Alex's nocturnal activities. "That's something you don't see very often. A woman washing a dog at 3 a.m."

But that was Alex. She probably enjoyed the bath more than the dog. The rental truck pulled out of Quincy on an already hot April day. As I whipped the big truck out of town we followed the Mississippi River north. I looked at the swollen banks that often flooded West Quincy and shifted west to Vietnam, thinking about the rice paddies that often flooded over. I wondered if I would ever stop thinking about Vietnam. I had left my job in Quincy earlier than I had to because I wanted to move to Minnesota before Alex had the baby, which was due on her mother's birthday, May 6.

She arrived at 1:11 p.m. on May 6, 1977. Amber was always on target, both on her arrival in this world and when she later scolded me on how to handle her and her younger brother Bryant.

We found a nice home like my parents' home in Sibley. It was covered by white stucco with an apple tree and a rock garden in the backyard. There were two bedrooms upstairs and two down so we thought we were ready for expansion.

Going back to school expanded my thinking. I had not decided for sure whether I wanted to teach English or Phy Ed, but I picked the former because I wanted to teach kids to think and write, not think and react. You were safe from harm in writing. In phy ed you could be injured. I had enough of injuries, both during and after Nam.

Probably the best part of the going back to school was that I was forced to face my feelings about Vietnam. The war had ended two years before. One class in particular was the opening of the floodgates of pain. Ironically, it was led by a former Vietnam war protestor, professor Dennis Trudell, who might have been apprehensive about having a Vietnam vet in his class. But he soon saw I was not a threat, but a resource. The course was on Vietnam literature and we read "Dispatches" by Michael Herr, which I could relate to because Herr was a war correspondent like me. Others like Philip Caputo's "A Rumor of War," about what Marines did under pressure, and Tim O'Brien's "Going After Cacciato," which was a dream-like sequence of events served to bring back both the reality and the nightmarish dreams I had of the country I left 10 years before. I had been greeted like a leper by the young people with their anti-war demonstrations.

But one of the students, Donna Klosterman from a small farming community called Blanchardville in neighboring Wisconsin, said that she considered me a Good Samaritan for trying to help my brother in Vietnam. She knew that was why I went in the first place. Others like Amy Klassy and Molly Shepard listened and thanked me with their soft smiles. One of the students was in the service. Johnny Borys had the look of a gung-ho Marine before Vietnam.Of course, if he had gone there, the look would have changed to disillusionment.

I zipped through the courses, not missing one class in the two years it took me to gain my teaching license and complete my student teaching assignment at Mukwonago High School, where I constantly reminded the students to never give up. I told them if I could make it through a war and not give up, then they should be able to hack their personal battles at home. Several of the kids I taught came from broken homes. I wondered how many of the kids had battle-scarred Vietnam vets for fathers. One of my top students, Chad Kuzbek, fit that scenario. His father had been there and his dad and mom were divorced. Yet he divorced himself from his parents' problems and excelled in the classroom. After completing my student teaching internship I had to find full time work, but there was no shortage of teachers and I fell into the role of a substitute teacher for two years before finding a job.

The pay was so poor that I considered many times leaving the teaching profession, but Chico Durand, who had moved next door to us in Bloomington, Minnesota, and now had become my closest friend, exercised his option to suggest, "Moses, you are doing a lot of good for a lot of kids in a lot of schools."

I hoped that was the case. The kids at the 10 schools I taught at loved the "Never give up" war stories I would share with them when the regular lesson was completed.

Although my teaching license covered high school and junior high, I would sometimes fill in at an elementary school. Those were places I did not tell my war stories. Because I had felt a purging of my feelings as I told the stories, I thought I had finally begun the healing process. I had suppressed the near-death experiences-no, probably buried them-and did not even share the "short-round" story with my wife. I told her about Troll, but not about me. I avoided my most terrifying moment like a new-found attack of cholera. Since I felt it not wise to discuss war stories with little kids, I felt cheated and would be in a surly mood when going to an elementary school. One day I was scheduled for Fredonia Elementary School and had put on my bad attitude right before showering and shaving and kissing my wife good-bye. I had decided today was going to be a bad day.

When I got to the school, I found out I had to share the duties with another teacher. I did not feel like sharing anything that day. The teacher was a bright, funny, lovely gal named Joyce, who overwhelmed me in the greeting.

"Mr. Moses, boy am I happy to have you here. Some of the boys have been getting out of hand in kindergarten lately and we need a man for these little guys to look up to. You look like you can handle anything."

Before I could reply, this tumultuous tornado, who looked like she could handle anything even though she was only a little over 5-foot tall, had whisked me down the hall. When she introduced me to the kids, they were all eyes and ears for this pint-sized instructor. I could see she did not need my help, but she wanted to make me feel at home and wanted to make sure I felt needed. I'll never forget her for her kindness.

When I arrived back from Vietnam I had not felt at home or needed. When I mentioned how I felt to Alex, she dismissed my argument.

"I think you're stretching the truth, Jock. Sure, some did not accept you, but you should know we all cared about you."

She was talking about both my family and hers. My older brother had circumnavigated the service by jumping on the education trail, finally ending the excursion with a doctor's degree in philosophy. He tried to use that philosophy in his work as a detective and he also used his anti-war philosophies on me. We battled about war, which was strange because we had grown up in the same house. Shouldn't we have the same feelings? While I soured on his attitude toward not supporting me for going, I later realized he was not against me, but against hurting others.

Therefore, we really wanted the same thing: to be able to live in a world where we spend time helping, not hurting others. Mistakenly, I had taken his reaction personally.

It was his wife, Kelley, who had gone to school with my brother Garner and had finished law school, and after a stint as a lawyer, had become a judge, who straightened me out about my brother. Whether it was her ability to argue as a lawyer or the desire to see two brothers resolve a conflict, I am not sure, but she guided me toward the conclusion even a hung jury couldn't refute.

"Don't you think your brother loves you?"

She answered for me. "Of course he does. He does not believe in war and I know you don't either. You may have gone there to do your duty. I know you think Garner should have welcomed you home with open arms. But the country was at war with itself at that time. Was the war right? Is war ever right? We had to come to grips with that question on an individual basis and none of us thought about the veterans it would hurt. That was wrong. Garner may be a detective, but even he has not found the key to tell you the ambivalent feelings for the war and for you. But I hope both of you will realize that you love each other as brothers."

The look on her face was oddly reminiscent of the warriors I had fought with in Vietnam. Strong-willed, Kelley was a warrior woman.

Love each other like brothers is what Kelley had said.

Garner had not been the only brother I had trouble loving. My friend Aaron had nearly disappeared out of my life it seemed. Of course, I had moved around so much that I was hard to follow. I wondered where Aaron and Moses would end up.

Would Aaron finish the race of life as the leader he was in Vietnam or as the gutter dweller that many vets had found as a resting place? Would I finally find a place I could call home and would I settle down in one job?

I went for help at a Vet Center meeting, but I was not like these guys, who had been married and divorced three times or had been a street person and a mental case for 10 years because they could not deal with the pain. I was happily married, but I dealt with the pain by ignoring it. I wasn't giving up on life like Aaron. But I wasn't any better than Aaron, either. I had not come face to face with my feelings about the horrible Asian war. And I knew Kelley was right. I had not felt it was a horrible war when I got on the Marine transport in 1966, but now, more than 20 years later, I knew it had been horrible.

I wished I could help Aaron, but he thought he was a failure or he would have called me. He had failed at climbing back into the U.S.A. structure, but he was not a failure, unless he gave up. His father and I would talk about him and we both believed in him, although I know he thought his father thought he was temporarily on the wrong path. Mr. Aaron also believed in the phrase my father had taught me and that was to never give up.

There was a breakthrough in our relationship a couple years before Mr. Aaron died.

"Pray for Junior," Mr. Aaron told me on one of our long-distance discussions about his son. "I took him down to a psychiatric hospital and found out he couldn't forgive himself for calling in artillery on women and children."

Then he added, "The doctor told me something else I didn't know, Jock. I think you should know this. Junior told the doctor that he once almost killed his best friend when he called in the wrong grid or something. I didn't understand. Do you?"

I had been sitting in a comfortable, albeit beat-up brown leather chair. I suddenly flashed back to an unforgettable night in 1967. I wasn't in a comfort zone that night. Aaron had made the mistake. I thought it had been a lieutenant, but apparently the officer had given him the right information and Aaron had communicated the wrong numbers to his artillery officer.

Aaron had almost killed me. I shuttered. I knew what I had to do.

Since my friend Aaron and his wife Maddy divorced it seemed as if our relationship became like the eroding shoreline of Florida. We were probably not even aware of how far our feelings had drowned in the aftermath of Vietnam. Maybe we were afraid to confront our feelings. I know I didn't want to talk about my experiences at first, but when I became a teacher and the kids wanted to hear about what it was like to be in a war, I was unable to stop the flow of information as the healing began. Since I had not talked to Aaron about our time in Vietnam and he did not care to discuss that time with me, we reached an impasse. But now I knew why he did not want to talk about that time. I knew why he drank himself into oblivion or took cocaine to disappear into a dream world. And what I had to do was tell him I understood. I wanted to tell him I cared about him and that I loved him like a brother-a brother in war.

If I could tell him that, would there be a miracle turn around for Aaron? I realized it might be too late, but if my kids could remember my credo-Never Give Up- than maybe I could impart that to Aaron.

CHAPTER 26

A second son is born

I had lived in Bloomington, a southern suburb of Minneapolis, for 10 years. Now I needed to find my southern friend. It was the spring of 1990. About seven months before Aaron's father's accident.

Ten years had whipped by faster than the new greyhound we had adopted. The decade was marked by the birth of our fourth child, our son Bryant. And by my pop's death in 1980. I wondered what the next decade would hold. Birth or death? Probably both. My oldest daughter had found a young man to love. His name was Ezra Palmer. Someone said once a girl marries a man like her father. Well, Palmer was a tall, right-handed pitcher in the Baltimore Orioles minor league system. So, I figured if these two got hitched, there would be a birth. But whose death?

I threw that ominous question into the back part of my computer brain, trying to forget death for awhile. After all, I wanted to start thinking positive thoughts as I ran after "Ponds," who once had been the cream of the crop in Vietnam, but in the U.S.A. he was just another black statistic.

I didn't want him to become a number. I wanted him to become a person who was worthwhile. But what did he want? I called his daughter and my Goddaughter Hope. She had moved to Milwaukee where "Ponds" had said he had relatives.

Hope had struggled just like her daddy, but she was trying to right herself. After getting pregnant in 10th grade, she had to quit school. But now she was about ready to take her G.E.D., a high school equivalency test that would give her a diploma. Then she was headed to college to become a nurse. I hoped she would make it. When I called, she was excited to hear my voice. Immediately I asked her about her father.

"He said he wanted to live with me because he had no place to live after he lost his job and his home. But I have to take care of myself first. I feel lost yet. I am trying to find the right direction."

I knew that my friend Aaron was lost. I had felt that way, too, when I failed at baseball and golf. But I never admitted that. After all, I was a fighter. I had this macho man attitude that did not allow me to feel lost. I wondered why that was. Why did I always have to battle life? When I thought about not battling life, about giving up, my thoughts went to Aaron.

"Where can I reach him, Hope? I want to tell him I haven't given up on him."

"I will call somebody and see if I can get you two together."

Apparently she wanted us to get together because she called back within two hours.

"Hello, godfather, I found out he's staying with a sister of a former girlfriend. He's hiding from his father because I know my grandfather does not approve of her kind."

I didn't take time to ask what "her kind" meant, but I knew my friend Aaron's father believed in having the right kind of friends. Because of my friend's track record since Vietnam I knew that the choices he had made in friends were a major cause of a road that had plummeted him into valleys that were full of the monsters of alcohol and other drugs.

"O.K., Hope, what's the number?"

"There's no phone. You'll have to go there. Here's the address." I wasn't that familiar with Milwaukee but I told her I'd find the place - and her father.

"Why don't you come and see me first?" she implored.

I took down her address and her phone number and said I would have to make arrangements for the trip.

"It's Easter vacation next week. Maybe I'll come then. I'll let you know."

When I thought about Easter I had conflicting feelings. Some people just considered the bunny, but since I was brought up in a Christian home, I reflected on Christ's death and resurrection. Those two concepts were conflicting to me, too. I thought of the deaths I had witnessed in war time. While many Marines had seen more buddies die than I had, seeing one friend die changes you-forever. I didn't always know what the friend's faith was so I did not know if I would see him again in heaven.

Now heaven is a conflicting subject to many too. My friend Aaron did not believe the same as his parents. My older brother was a lot like Aaron in that they wanted a Gandhi-type peace in the world, one that I could never see coming. Was there peace in my friend Aaron's life now? I was soon to find out because I had decided to drive the nearly 400 miles to Milwaukee to see him.

I didn't know what to expect because of his daughter's comment about not wanting him to live with her.

"I have enough problems of my own," she had told her father.

Aaron's father had always bailed him out of trouble. He never had to suffer the natural consequences. Maybe if Mr. Aaron had let that happen...

CHAPTER 27

How my brother had changed

Aaron. I almost didn't recognize him. The dignified gentleman who had stood up in my wedding decades ago was gone. Replacing him was a stoop shouldered, taciturn, battered man.

Life had left him. It was almost like looking at a ghost. The spirit, the substance had gone. Tarnished, disheveled, he opened the door.

The smile came.

But it was not the same tantalizing one that used to hook me.

It was hollow.

The smile.

"Moses, what are you doing here?"

It was at that point that he may have wished he could have broken down crying and asked for my help.

But he didn't. He had been taught to be proud by his father, whether he had a reason to be or not. He gathered himself, raised his head and trying to stand tall he asked me in.

In the next two hours we talked about a lot of things. But like the genius he was, he never talked about the fix he was in.

What could I do? I could listen.

I found a moment to tell the woman who was in the house- a sister of a woman who he lived with after divorcing Maddy- that I needed to know what was going on. She could have blown me off, but somehow she figured Aaron and Moses were brothers and I might help. She told me that Aaron had been charged with drunken driving right after coming to Milwaukee and was in danger of losing his license. Did I know of a lawyer?

I did.

Alexandra's brother Sawyer had in-laws in Milwaukee. One of his relatives was a lawyer. I remember Sawyer saying you could always find him because his photo was in the Sunday papers in the classified ads. I asked this woman if she had a Sunday paper.

She did.

There in front of me was an answer to prayer-Webster Courtland, drunken driving lawyer pictured with a slick hairdo and neatly trimmed beard. I wondered how slick he was and how neatly he could trim any sentence that might be imposed on Aaron.

I called the number in the city's paper, the Milwaukee Journal.

"This is the office of the best drunken driving lawyer in the city," said a pleasant voice on the phone. "Can I help you?"

I had to laugh at the veracity of the receptionist for her boss, but I hoped her assessment was accurate.

"What's your name? You sure know how to introduce a guy."

"My name is Daniela and I wouldn't be here if I didn't know how to uplift the man.   So, do you want to talk to Mr. Courtland?"

"You bet. Is he in, Daniela?"

"I will check, Mr.-what did you say your name was?"

"Moses."

"All right, Mr. Moses, I believe he is with a client."

I wondered if all lawyers were always with a client when their secretaries or receptionists said they were or if that was a stock line to make you think lawyers were in demand.

The answer was obvious because Daniela was back to me in a flash.

"He said he will be with you in two shakes of a lamb's tail, Mr. Moses."

Again I figured that line was to keep me on the line, but it wasn't too long before I was talking to Webster

Courtland and pleading with him to take the case of a friend.

After giving Courtland the details, he said he would defend Aaron. Then he said something that I thought lawyers didn't do.

Actually it was a question Courtland asked.

"What can your friend Aaron afford to pay?"

"Don't you have a standard fee?" I asked him.

"Never have. I get rich off the rich and scale my fees down from there. You know what I mean, Mr. Moses?"

"Well, Aaron is a Vietnam vet..." I started, not knowing why I began with that description or what that past time in his life had specifically to do with the present. I told him he had just moved to Milwaukee and was lost in many ways, not just financially.

"This guy needs help, Mr. Courtland."

"When is his court date?"

I had not found that out, but told Courtland I would dig it up.

"That won't be necessary. I will check the court calendar. Tell your friend to call me or come see me before the court date, though."

I explained that he did not have a phone or a car.

We arranged a meeting when I said I would bring Aaron in for a consultation.

Courtland was brilliant enough to realize Aaron needed more than to beat a drunken driving charge. In fact,

Courtland made sure he did not receive a fine, but was ordered to receive help from A.A.

Aaron went to Alcoholics Anonymous for the next six months and was able to drive a cab part time on work release. Courtland had a friend who gave him the temporary job. I went back home and prayed all would be well with him. While Mackenzie Aaron, Jr. didn't do any more drinking and driving and finished his sentence and went home to Augusta about a month before Thanksgiving, it was that mistake- a man drinking and driving- that put Mackenzie Aaron, Sr. in a coma.

I was glad that my friend Aaron had not put anyone in the hospital. After seeing his father lay in the hospital bed, I realized the pain drinking and driving could cause. I realized how Billy Golenbock had died.

I realized it could have happened to both Aaron and I or to someone we could have injured.

CHAPTER 28

Mr. Aaron's funeral

I was jarred back to the present. The television meteorologist said a winter storm warning was still in effect. Six to eight inches was expected. We always had plenty of snow in Minnesota. When I was a boy in Sibley, we once visited my Aunt Isabelle's farm in St. James in southern Minnesota, where the snow plows had piled up the snow as high as the telephone lines.

But by the end of March you'd figure Old Man Winter was done. After all, spring had officially started yesterday.

Mr. Aaron no longer laid in a hospital bed. Dolly had told me he had died of heart failure. I couldn't believe it. This man had waved at me to tell me he was coming back to life only four months before. Maybe the great effort he made trying had been too hard on a 72-year-old heart. Dolly had not really explained what happened.

The church was packed for the funeral. I took Alex and our youngest son Bryant, who was in kindergarten, to Augusta for the funeral. The pastor asked if anyone wanted to say anything about Mr. Aaron.

Since I had never been bashful, I jumped up and quickly walked to the stained-glass front where a light landed on the closed casket. I was glad the casket was closed, because I wanted to remember Mr. Aaron alive, not dead.

With tears streaming down my cheeks, I told the mostly black-faced audience that I felt like the character Jody in John Steinbeck's "The Red Pony." I said he "marched seemingly alone, with high-lifted knees and pounding feet, but behind...there was a phantom army with great flags and swords, silent but deadly." I told them that Mr. Aaron's army included the sons he taught, which I felt included me. Then I looked at my friend Aaron.

I wanted to say something about us, but I couldn't find the words. Maybe later I could tell him.

Friends from other churches were also in attendance.

Father York, a priest, was in attendance. I felt that was unusual for a Catholic father to be present at a Protestant funeral. But then Mr. Aaron was able to jump religious hurdles as well as break the color barriers.

The Ivys were also there. The Ivys were one of the first families to break through a tough obstacle- the Iron

Curtain. Mr. Aaron knew what it was like to break through the iron curtains of prejudice. John Ivy was founder of The Open Door, an organization which had brought Bibles to families in Czechoslovakia and the Ukraine. The richest family in Sibley was the Marshalls and Mr. Marshall had been instrumental in funding The Open Door's medical as well as spiritual projects. When I told Mr. Aaron about The Open Door and what they were doing he got involved too by convincing his home church to add to the Marshall plan for the disadvantaged. I thought what Mr. Aaron's church was doing was slightly ironic. One disadvantaged group-the black population- helping a primarily white population in sore need of help way across the world. They were successful. Yet when a predominantly white nation like the U.S. tried to help a poor nation like Vietnam it didn't work out.

Also present at the funeral was Stan Hope, a Quaker leader from Rocky Hollow, Pennsylvania, who Mr. Aaron had met in Washington, D.C., when both were trying to help elderly people who had been forgotten by Congress. So, here was a Baptist deacon being honored by a Catholic priest, a Quaker leader and even a world-wide evangelist. And by one Lutheran Marine from Minnesota.

After the funeral I hoped to renew old acquaintances with Aaron. But first I had to take time with the family at a dinner.

Aaron's oldest brother was only a couple weeks away from election day. But if he was thinking about that important day, it was not apparent. He was busy greeting everyone, playing the role of No. 1 son, not candidate for mayor.

Thanks to the voting act of 1965 black men could ascend to become a mayor of Atlanta. Richard Hatcher had blazed the way to become the first black mayor of a major city in 1967, when Aaron and I were blazing the way through the jungles of Vietnam. Really neither one of us blazed any trails in Nam. We were not heroes. Aaron had spent his time inside a command post calling out numbers for fire missions. I had spent my time writing about what happened in those fire missions. I remembered back to a February night when a short round ended one life and almost took mine. I wondered if Aaron had come to grips with that nightmare. I would ask him later.

I talked with Dolly for awhile. We talked about her-our-father.

"Why did you transfer him to Atlanta?" I asked.

"He needed the best care, Jock. My father always wanted the best for us. I know I gave him grief by not always listening to his ideas, but I guess they sank in even when I was trying to block out his wisdom."

"What's happening with Junior?"

"When he came home after the trouble in Milwaukee, he continued his associations with some old friends, the wrong kind if you know what I mean."

"I can't understand it, Dolly. This guy never listened to others in the Marines. He was a leader. Others listened to him. Even I did."

"Daddy used to say he might have been better off staying under the structure of the Marines. He had found his niche there, but I guess no one knew that at the time.

"I have tried to contact him many times over the years and he always seems to avoid me. Does he think I have made it and he didn't? What's the story?"

"Jock, don't put what's happened to Junior on yourself. Junior did to Junior. You have nothing to do with his life. He had choices. He made the wrong ones. You've made the right ones."

I wasn't so sure about her black-and-white assessment of Aaron's and Moses' lives. Certainly Aaron had not always been wrong and certainly I had not always been right. But maybe that was the way my friend Aaron thought.

Maddy was seated with her two girls. I wondered if she felt strange being around her former husband.

She told me that she was moving to Stone Mountain near Atlanta to prepare for the Olympics which was coming to that city in 1996. She was having a house built, which would be ready in another year.

"I will be marketing homes where people can stay when they come to the Olympics. It will be a grand project."

I changed the subject.

"I really feel sorry that things didn't work out for you and 'Ponds.'"

She may have felt sorry, too, but she masked that with her retort.

"You know, Jock, I don't even think about him anymore."

I had the feeling Maddy, my friend Aaron's sister Dolly, and his brothers didn't want to think much about him. I felt they felt he had disgraced the family. Yet he was there at the funeral. The twins, Quincy and Tavish, were nowhere to be seen that day. I thought that was disgraceful. But nobody mentioned it in the Aaron clan. The dinner was over. I went upstairs from the basement where the dinner had been served. I told Alex that I was going to talk to Aaron.

Aaron was with Miles. They were planning to party that night.

"That's rather thoughtless, isn't it?" I said. " I mean, how can you party on the same day as your father's funeral?"

"Lighten up, little brother," said Aaron in a tone I had heard before. He had always been the strong one in our relationship.

"There is nothing we can do about my father now. Listen, how about you ditching your wife and son and coming over to this motel we're renting for the night?"

I had reservations about saying yes, but I felt drawn to my friend.

Nothing had changed that. Not the years we had spent apart. Not my trouble with jobs or his trouble with drugs and alcohol. Our friendship was still there as far as I was concerned. I wasn't sure he had always wanted our friendship to continue, although now he was saying he wanted to spend some time with me in a critical time. And I wanted to ask him about that night in Vietnam.

I told Alex to go back to our motel and not wait up for me.

There was a crowd already present when we got to the motel room. There was a suite of rooms, but there was nearly wall-to-wall people anyway. When I went to Aaron's haunts, of course, they were attended by 100 percent blacks, or almost always. That never bothered me. I knew there was a difference in color skin, but "Ponds" skin color never mattered to me.

Mrs. Aaron's words from years ago came floating into my mind.

"You know, Jock, Junior has a lot of acquaintants, but you're the only friend he has really ever had."

I didn't feel like I had been a friend to him over the years. When he had gone into a psychiatric ward his father had told me about it and I could have visited him, but I never did. I felt I let him down in a critical time.

But I hoped I could make it up to him in the years to come. The booze flowed freely that night. Plenty of malt liquor melted the inhibitions of the previously solemn

250

occasion of the funeral, which had taken place only five hours before.

Aaron was talking to a statuesque, golden-haired girl named Audrey, who was the only other white inhabitant present that night. I watched Aaron smile. He used to be a handsome man, I thought. His smile not only showed a mouthful of dental problems, but also portrayed how he had not taken care of himself.

I figured he was trying to hustle this slick chick because she was almost as tall as he was. Aaron's smile once would have melted any girl's heart, but that time had past. She shook her head and moved away. I moved in.

He counterpunched with a surprise. He called me by my Vietnam nickname, which he had not done since we had returned to the States. Was he back in Vietnam mentally? I soon found out he felt split between Asia and the America. He was lost.

"Heh, Granny, what's happening? Now, don't you think my father would like to be here himself?"

I thought of the double meaning that question had. I knew his father was dead, but if he had been alive he would probably rather be dead than caught alive at this booze party. I had never seen Mr. Aaron drunk. I knew Mr. Aaron would be sad to see his son in the condition he was in. But I remembered what my father had said when I was 10 and had just struck out.

CHAPTER 29

"When you're knocked down, get up to fight again."

When you're knocked down, get up to fight again. What I mean, Jock, is to never give up."

My father had been dead for 10 years, and that memory was almost 40 years old, but I could zoom back to my father alive and his golden apples of wisdom in a flash.

I thought that my pop meant not to give up on friends as well as myself. I could have given up on myself. Falling short of the majors in baseball, flunking the golf test, and not finding a teaching job for two years after I received my license were three good reasons to quit. But my pop's face smiled at me, with those scars of living enveloped by that smile, and I realized I couldn't quit.

And I wasn't going to give up on my friend Aaron.

When I first looked in his face a quarter of a century before I had seen a giant who had asked me to quiet down. Now I was looking at a midget who I hoped to quiet down.

He had always been "cool" when he drank before, but that, too, had changed. He became loud and abrasive that night, maybe because he was searching for ways to vent the loss of a father, who he thought didn't love him because of the way his life had turned out. I knew his father had loved him dearly. But I also knew Mackenzie Aaron, Jr. had missed those loving feelings.

"You know, Granny, I can't remember Vietnam anymore."

"I don't believe that, Ponds." (I called him by his Nam nickname to help him remember.) "How about that night PFC Green was killed by a short round, one that almost nailed me in a pine box forever? I bet you remember that! Don't you?"

My friend Aaron's face exploded.

"How the hell did you know that?"

Before I could answer, he fired another blast at me.

"My father told you, didn't he? When I was in the psych ward, I told him I was ashamed of my time in Nam. I almost killed my best friend."

He had never called me his "best" friend before, but he didn't have to.   But it was nice to hear him call me that anyway.

"Of course I remember that, Granny. I have never been able to forget it. I have been running away from that night for a long time. Every time I see you I realized what I could have done. I hate you, man."

He ran out of the room. He was escaping again. It had been alcohol and other drugs which had fueled his escapes before. It was happening again.

I followed him.

I was afraid for my friend Aaron.

Miles was giving life his best by singing along with a Sixties tune by Mitch Jagger and the Rolling Stones called "I Can't Get No Satisfaction," that was coming out of a black boom box in the corner.

"I'm going out after Junior," I told Miles as I shifted into second gear and ran out the door to the Garden of Eden Motel.

My friend Aaron had gone to the edge of the street, under a street light that had burned out.

The night was full of love and hate. He had called me his best friend and than had said he hated me.

"Ponds, I'll never give up on you, man. There's still hope. I love you like a brother."

He heard what I said, but like seeds that fall among thorns they did not bear fruit because the alcohol choked his mind.

"You're not my brother. You never will be."

He ran into the street.

Maybe because of the streetlight that was out the driver of the car didn't see Ponds. The front bumper slammed into my friend's body, hurdling him airborne for what seemed like a lifetime. Then his massive frame slammed into the street. His head cracked against the pavement. I can still hear that sound.

I felt like everything was happening in slow motion. I wanted to run the fastest of my life to help my friend Aaron. But I was in shock. I could not move.

My friend Aaron lay in total silence just like his father had months before.

The paramedics said they thought he was dead when his head hit the concrete.

He had said that I, Jock Moses, was not his brother.

But Mackenzie Aaron, Jr., was wrong.

He was my brother.

But that argument was laid to rest for the time being because suddenly Aaron gasped, striving to prove the paramedics' death diagnosis wrong. "Heh," I yelled at the paramedic, who seemed as tall as the Washington Monument as I looked up at him from street level. "My friend is alive."

In shock, the monumental statement shook the paramedic as he dropped the phone he was holding. He had just called to inform the hospital of a death. Now, he had to almost apologetically say they would be transporting a corpse who had come back to life.

"I don't believe it," said the giant paramedic to his friend, who was a foot shorter than he was. Kinda like Aaron and Moses, I thought.

"You stupid ..." the shorter paramedic started and then thought better of finishing the sentence. He whispered, "On the job a week and this is the second time you have made that mistake." The shorter medic did not think I had heard that, but I had even though my hearing was impaired from the short round many years before.

I got up with a vengeance, then realized he was young. All at once, I knew what would have an effect on him. Was I beginning to think before I acted? Must be a sign of growing up. Nah, never happen, I thought.

I grabbed the tall paramedic by the shirt and my fist started toward his chin but stopped inches short of his jaw.

"I should beat the snot out of you, but I have a feeling you'll never make the same mistake three times. I love baseball and you know three strikes you're out. I am filing a report on you because you have to be accountable. But I hope it will help you be a better paramedic."

What was I saying? Were these the lines of a friend who had almost lost his best friend from Nam. This guy almost let Aaron die! I blasted him in the mouth. The blood went flying like a torn cover off a baseball. And I knew I had just broken my hand.

Tears came down the face of the tall dude. He was sorry. He would never forget his mistake. When my hand swelled up like an overstuffed tomato it was a signal to the other paramedic I needed first aid, too.

"Nice right hand, man," he smiled as he grabbed a sack of ice and wrapped the bag around my hand. "Climb in the back."

Several hours later at the hospital I found out that Aaron had a blood clot and he would need an operation to relieve the pressure.

By now my buddy had become conscious and when he found out what was happening asked me something he had never asked me before.

"Would you pray for me, man?" Aaron intoned in that soft bass voice of his.

I nodded. The words that came out of my mouth were from another source.

"Dear Heavenly Father, I love my brother here. He needs strength right now. Bring him through this surgery. Guide the hands of the doctors and nurses. Thank you Jesus. I know you have promised you would answer prayer if we just ask. Amen, brother."

Aaron didn't say anything. He just closed his eyes as the attendants like dutiful waiters at a restaurant wheeled the cart away. But this cart was not full of dessert for the end of the meal; it was full of a man who almost missed the end of his life.

I went looking for the coffee machine after the nurse said the surgery would take four hours. "You can go home," she said.

"No, I belong here with my friend."

"Odd," she said.

"Waddya mean?"

"You don't see many black and white guys who are friends these days."

With my back up like an alley cat ready to do battle, I said. "So you think it's odd, eh?"

She saw the anger on my face.

"No, no, I don't mean it's not O.K. You are certainly in the minority."

I cracked up at her saying I was in the minority.

"Good joke," I said, "me in the minority."

She laughed too.

"How long have you been friends?"

"Since Vietnam. Long time. We've been through tough times, both together and separately. I had my dream of making the big leagues in baseball shattered and then had more than a dozen jobs since then. My friend has had problems with drinking and drugs. He's divorced."

"And you?

"Are you divorced, too?"

"No," I said emphatically. "I thank God I have a wife that has hung with me through thick and thin. The only time she couldn't hack it was when they had to peel me off a picket fence after I leaped for a baseball."

"Ouch. You said you thank God. Are you a Christian?"

"Well, at least I think I am."

This nurse smiled that peaceful smile Jeff Grotenhuis had and probably his Aunt Bonnie had. "You can know...what's your name?"

"Moses. Jock Moses."

"Well, Moses, Jock Moses, you can know you are a Christian. I was just reading in my Bible this morning in I John 5:13 where the writer says, 'I write these things to you that believe in the name of the son of God that you may know you have eternal life.' When you say you think you're a Christian you're saying you think you have to be good enough, right?"

She didn't wait for me to answer.

"No one is good enough or perfect enough. Are you perfect?"

Again she didn't wait for an answer.

"Of course not. No one is. But if you rely on what Jesus did, you are a follower of Jesus and a follower of Jesus Christ is called a Christian, right?

"So, keep smilin' brother. You can know today you are going to heaven."

She stopped the river of words that cascaded over me like no other words had ever affected me.

I knew she was right.

My parents had imparted those beliefs deep within my soul years before. Through chasing a dream to be a major league star, I had missed who was in charge of my life. It wasn't me. It wasn't even Billy Golenbeck, my favorite manager in my baseball life. It was God almighty as Mrs.

Aaron always referred to the creator of the mountains in New Hampshire and the lakes in Minnesota and more importantly the creator of Aaron and Moses.

I knew it would be a long night. I looked at the nametag on this nurse's uniform. "Bo, where could I find some rest?"

"I think you know where the permanent rest is now, Moses. But you can go in this room that is not occupied. I'll wake you up at 7."

She led me through the open door and I kicked off my sneakers and my head started toward the pillow.

I fell asleep before my head hit the target.

When I woke up I could not see a thing. No one else was in the room.It was so dark in the room that I panicked momentarily. I felt like I was in a coffin. I saw a clock attached to the ceiling that read 7:00. Bo was just coming through the door as I rolled out of the bed.

My panic dissipated and I left for the surgical floor. Aaron's surgery was over. When I reached the floor where Aaron had been operated on, they said he had been moved.

I thought they were lying. I thought Aaron had died and they wouldn't tell me. "He's dead, isn't he? You won't tell me the truth. I'll find the truth."

The tag said "unit assistant" on the nurse's blouse. She quickly showed she was no assistant to anyone. "Listen. I always tell the truth. Don't you understand. He's been moved to intensive care. That's one floor down, OK!"

I bounced down the stairs like a football player running through a tire drill.

"How is he?"

"Who?"

"My brother?"

"Your brother?"

"Yea. Aaron MacKenzie, Jr."

This woman started to giggle, then couldn't hold it and split up with laughter.

"Sorry," she said," but we don't usually have brothers in here that are as different as you and your brother!"

She cracked up again, leaning back in her chair, grabbing unto both sides to keep from falling out of her seat.

"You are such a small man and he's tall. And the obvious black-and white issue? Think about it."

I smiled, but forgot to laugh. I had been through a lot in the last few hours, most of which was like a bad movie that you were forced to watch.

This lady of laughs shook her gray-haired head, adjusted her glasses. "He's behind that curtain over there. He's O.K. He has other visitors." I felt like the father in the story "'Twas the Night Before Christmas" as I threw upon the curtain and looked for Santa Claus and what presents he brought.

I didn't find any white-bearded man, but a black man in white gauze wrapped around his head like an Egyptian mummy. His new lady Shirley was there with her daughter from a previous marriage. I had met them both before at the funeral of Junior's father. Junior talked first.

"Heh, Jock."

"You're all right."

"Yea."

The smile came, one that used to show beautiful rows of ivory but now showed a rotting row of displaced dentistry.

Yes, I thought, he's all right. But for how long I wondered.

"Jock, thanks for praying for me before. Would you pray with me now?"

This time I was the one with tears streaming down my face. After knowing this man for a quarter of century that was one thing we had never done. I knew his father and mother would have loved to been there at that moment.This time I moved closer. To pray. Aaron and Moses.

We were brothers. I knew that. Now he knew that, too.

It had taken an accident to bring us both to this spot. Maybe his brains had been scrambled to the right texture for God to move in and change his heart as well as his thinking process.

He was out of the hospital in a month. The medical brains wanted to make sure everything was intact and Aaron's brains would not swish to one side or another like a shaken snow storm in a globe that a son buys for his mother.

But the battle was not over. My friend Aaron did not go back to drugs despite living in the same old haunts.

He went into the V.A. Hospital to "get the cure."

He followed the rules and was soon back in an apartment in an area where getting a hit had nothing to do with baseball. There wasn't much grass where he lived with Shirley and their 10-year-old daughter Victoria.

Only asphalt.

No man is an island said John Donne.

Aaron MacKenzie, Jr. was no exception. His father and mother brought him up right. Many folks had continued to pray for him through the past 25 years. For the last 15 years since a grand old lady friend of mine named Muggy Hagen asked me to start a prayer list like her husband had before he died I had been typing in names of those I loved. My friend Aaron was first on the list since I had placed the names alphabetical because I knew God had no favorites. Weren't all men were alike to Him? Didn't everyone count?

CHAPTER 30

"Don't leave me now."

I made a trip to Atlanta again five months later. I had come to his upstairs apartment to go to a Braves baseball game and to bring him clothes from Goodwill that my bargain-hunting wife Alexandra had purchased for him. He was reading some "deep" book about the evolution vs. creation argument.

"You know I consider myself a prolific reader," said Aaron. "You know, so I can figure out life. These guys say that evolution is possible but don't back the stories up with the facts. Now, creation I figure is backed up by God."

He stopped, looked at me, knowing my eyes had just widened considerably.

Aaron kept going. "I used to tutor one of my friends in high school who is now a music professor at Florida A&M University. Even though I didn't get past the tenth grade, I did get my G.E.D. and have 2 1/2 years of college and want to teach history if I can go back and finish my schooling.

"Still, though," he reflected, "all this reading has not given me the answers to life."

He scratched his goatee, rose and said, "Let's go."

That night at the Braves game I asked him if he was ready to go back to the Christian beliefs he had learned from his father and mother as a little boy. I got out this pocket Bible I had with me and said John 3:16 was meant for him. "For God so loved the world that he gave his only begotten Son that whoever-that's you Ponds (using his name from Vietnam)-believes in him should not perish but have eternal life. Are you ready to believe that?" I asked.

"No," he said, looking straight ahead.

I thrust my Bible into my jacket and shut up. I knew he was close. He knew he did not have the answers. I felt he knew Jesus did.

The next time I saw him the leaves had changed colors and the college football season was in full swing. I had secured a job as a church consultant with a company called United where we ministered to churches by taking portraits of their families and put them into a memory book or album. One of our biggest churches we had served was First Baptist in Atlanta and I wanted to find out how things worked from the local church consultant. I had found a job in the Milwaukee area. I hoped it would be my last. Despite my exciting news I wanted to share with Aaron about my job, he had more important news for me. He told me he had received Christ as Lord and Savior of his life. "I didn't do it at the ballpark because I would have been doing it for you. I wanted to do it for me. Now I have."

We both got up from the green leather chairs we were sitting in his upstairs flat and embraced. A river of tears rolled down my face. He said softly, "Thanks, man. I knew you'd never give up on me. Don't leave me now, Jock."

He knew this was the beginning of a new life. The year was 1993.

What has happened to my friend Aaron since then?

Well, he found a job where he worked with monstrous electrical boxes and the management there saw his leadership. And the company asked him to go to China to help build stuff across the pond. But more importantly he's building a better life by going to Canaan Baptist Church every Sunday with his wife and daughter. Victoria loved going to Sunday school and pretty soon mother was going and then her father followed suit. And Aaron had a fine suit to go to church in since Alexandra found one for him. He looked really glad because he had a changed heart that made his smile broaden to a new dimension. In fact, you could see the love of Jesus in his face. And you know what he has done? He has started a drug rehab program called

Free and One, which translated means free from drugs and one in Christ.

Now I could say what happened next with me-Moses- and my friend Aaron. But that's another story. It's been more than 40 years wandering in the wilderness now. Both of us are scarred, but both of us know the right path to take. We're okay. I can tell you this. We will be hitting the wall again. But when we get knocked down like NBA star Dwyane Wade does so many times we will rise up to do battle with life just like he does and like our earthly fathers taught us to do. Why? Because we had and always will have our heavenly father with us.

We have confidence because we can both say, He is our father.

The end

88849737R00149

Made in the USA
Lexington, KY
18 May 2018